HORROR IN ARCHITECTURE

Joshua Comaroff and Ong Ker-Shing

"When abstraction sets about killing you,
you had better get busy."

Albert Camus, *The Plague*

"There is no exquisite beauty without
some strangeness in the proportions."

E.A. Poe, *Ligeia*

CONTENTS

Introduction

Typologies Of Horror

Postscript

Notes

Introduction

Sublime Horror

"Does a firm perswasion that a thing is so, make it so?"
William Blake[2]

Why spend time on horrifying things? Isn't life difficult enough? Antonio Rocco, as early as 1635, argued that we should look at problematic subjects because they are instructive. And because their opposite, anodyne beauty, contains a dangerous surfeit of sweetness.[3] Deviance teaches; charm will make you sick. Rocco claimed that horrors in particular—putrefaction, decay, distortion and dissymmetry among others—are sites of fertility, change, and invention.

In the case of architecture, horror appears particularly urgent. Firstly, because its experience is immanent in the project of the modern—it closely shadows the disconcerting scalar and typological growth of our built environment. Second, because its unique character is increasingly relevant in what we might call an "age of affect," in an emergent politics of the sublime where the ecstatic and the shocking pose as alternatives to older Enlightenment values. Thirdly—and not least— because horror is terribly effective in queering the assumptions of contemporary design practice. It deserves to be rehabilitated, because its violence is useful. It is a kind of Nietszchean operation. Its gleeful dismemberments, its deviant physicality, oppose the creep of reification and the comfort of well-tempered surfaces. To put it another way: horror is the truth about abstraction.

Certainly, horror prods the bounds of the thinkable. The horrible, like the mad, presents the world as it *might* be. It is utopianism without utopia, planning without plans. It speaks of the present in the future tense, and through a kind of inversion—like the words of a fool, it is that which can not be said under normal circumstances.

This is due, in part, to a unique historical ambivalence. Horror is an aesthetic category that has traditionally been home to profound skepticism about the merits of the aesthetic itself. From Roman times through the early nineteenth century, it was posited as a category distinct from either beauty or ugliness.[4] For Immanuel Kant, and the Romantics, it was an element of the sublime, experienced for spiritual and didactic benefit—a mode of feeling that would skirt rationality and speak directly to our inner nature. The *terrible* was one form of sublimity, alongside the *noble* and the *splendid*. Into the former camp goes objects that "arouse enjoyment but with horror."

The gravity of this is opposed to the sense of beauty, which was for Kant a much more superficial thing. In its simplicity and its greatness, by contrast, the sublime "moves."[5] This distinction recalls Longinus, originator of the concept, for whom the sublime tears up facts "like a thunderbolt."[6] Sublimity is superior precisely because it need not engage the faculties of persuasion. It is a *sensation*; when the sublime strikes, like pain or mortal fear, we simply *know* it to be true.[7] In the eighteenth century, Thomas Reid noted that this mode of communication "carries the hearer along with it involuntarily, and by a kind of violence than by cool conviction."[8] Indeed, this impressive horror is uncool. It is a site of swooning, of spiritual overpowering, of renewed commitments.

It is also a slippery fish; the great works on the subject continually remind one of its illuminating moral power, the value of clarified affect. In its wake, we will feel and know. But know what? For Kant, the "rigid" and "astonished" sensation revealed nothing less than the dignity of humanity itself. Sensing the sublime is an ethical operation—recognition of this dignity would spur one toward noble actions. This was not an unheard-of idea at the time. The British writers of moral sensitivity and improvement, such as the Third Earl of Shaftesbury and Lord Kames, also proposed that there were objects in the world capable of bettering their observers. For others, the sublime clearly invoked the religious. Erich Auerbach, for example, thought that Dante's description of the striding god who "passes the Stygian ferry with soles unwet"[9] succeeded in viscerally conjuring the power of divinity. Among contemporary evangelicals, for whom the sublime is alive and well as an affective discourse of faith and "spirit movement," it is the popular belief in the "evidence of things unseen." Horror is the shadow of the metaphysical, moving across the waters. In a word, it is God.

Well, a *form* of Him. But a rarefied and somewhat perverse one, occupying a moment in which the tidy beauty of nature begins to wear at the seams, and the unruly side—divine excess—expresses itself. This announces its presence in the impenetrable dark tangle of the valley floor, in split and sundered trees, in mountains "unjust" and "hook-shouldered," and in the nimbus pregnancies of stormy skies. In the two centuries following Nicolas Despréaux-Boileau's 1674 translation of Longinus, godly surplus was seen in the appreciation of "a wild element, something different from regularity."[10] This was famously

true for Jean-Jacques Rousseau, hence his heroic standing among French Romantics. But it was more commonly the taste of the English writers, such as John Dennis, and Thomas Burnet—who caught glimmers of this ferocious power in art more generally.

This nature was not the charming pastorals of the previous century, but something more appalling. In 1753, for example, Dr. John Brown wrote of Keswick in the English Lake District that:

> [its] perfection consists of three circumstances: Beauty, Horror and Immensity united…But to give you a complete idea of these three perfections, as they are joined in Keswick, would require the united powers of Claude, Salvator, and Poussin. The first should throw his delicate sunshine over the cultivated vales. The second should dash out the horror of the rugged cliffs, the steeps, the hanging woods, and foaming waterfalls; while the grand pencil of Poussin should crown the whole with the majesty of the impending mountains.[11]

Similarly, Thomas Gray wrote about a 1739 visit to a "monstrous precipice, almost perpendicular," which contained within itself "religion and poetry."[12] Joseph Addison had famously remarked that the Alps overtook him with an "agreeable type of horror," as he absorbed "one of the most irregular misshapen scenes of the world."[13] Burnet likewise praised those natural vistas "ill-figur'd" and "confused."[14]

Enrico Baj, Ultracorpo in Svizzera, 1959

Again, the emphasis here is not on the aesthetic, so much as the sensational: the eye becomes, in a very real *sense*, the window to the soul. In his influential article on the picturesque, Edmund Burke further clarified the effects of "sublime horrors." The arch conservative noted that the latter led to a condition of astonishment, that "state of the soul in which all emotions are suspended, with some degree of horror."[15] In contrast to beauty, the sensation of the sublime involves physical pain; it is aesthetics made anatomical. Sheer ugliness, by contrast, is more closely related to beauty. As Burke was quick to point out, these may share formal characteristics, such as proper proportion. By contrast, the sublime emerges from an unrelated matrix of sense, and can not be meaningfully compared.

For Burke, the painful fear inherent in the sublime is quickly converted to pleasure, as we realize that we are not in actual danger. It is sublimated in relief. In this sense, the phenomenal arc of the sublime resembles Kant's. The ache of fear, for the German Idealist, is dispelled via the dignity of the mind, which in this moment recognizes its own power. At the same time, this formulation oddly shadows Freud's explanation of laughter: it is "cathexic" energy that builds up anxiously, only to be released in a sort of exhalation. Such an effect was already theorized in Aristotle's *Poetics*, in a similar picture of catharsis. Fear (*eleos*) is one of the emotions thought to be provoked by literary art, and also ritually dispelled in a moment of social pleasure. Such an idea might help to explain some oddities we will encounter later: for example, the compound genre of comedy-horror in early American films, such as *The Cat and the Canary* (1927), *The Last Warning* (1929) and later in the *Scream* franchise.

But how the mighty have fallen. Since the late 19th century, horror has largely been exiled to the titillations of low culture, and to certain strains of art where it resonates unnamed. It has become that most mediocre of things, a "genre:" an area of production below the threshold of serious culture.[16] This divestment takes place against a backdrop of desacralization, and the creep of the banal into charismatic experience. Or, at least, the eviction of myth to new quarters. Theodor Adorno, for example, denied the continued existence of fear in art. Such terror was totemistic, the hallmark of a lost, enchanted age. It survived only as a feeling of discomfort, inherent in the repulsion of ugliness. The Frankfurt School theorist even went so far as to reject the kitsch character of that popular art—such as Vietnam protest songs—which attempted to "take the horrendous and make it somehow consumable."[17] For Adorno, horror was something "out there," in the world of imperialism, of Auschwitz, and the irrational.

Regardless, the ache of a de-spiritualized world has haunted this discourse, doggedly, for centuries. It was certainly felt in the age of the Romantics. In the work of Burke, as well as Lord Byron and Caspar David Friedrich, we are already aware of a groping for intensity of experience. Like the famous Claude Glass that was used to make picturesque landscapes more picturesque, this aspiration was ridiculed in its own time as dangerously over-ripe, an attempt to stage artificial emotive experiences. Sublime horror was understood as a mad grasp at something visceral, a kind of "emo" gesture toward unmediated feeling.

The Romantic courtship of sensation was likewise powerful in a society less overstimulated than our own. In contemporary culture, horror becomes merely one source,

among many, of "cheap thrills." Its effects are perhaps
blunted alongside cable news, video games simulating
mass killing, pornography, *Venti* coffees, and militarized
foods like "Krunchers," which can deliver a payload of 100
decibels directly into the inner ear for an "extreme" eating
experience.[18] Such titillation is understood by theorists
(and deplorers) of the modern condition as a means to
prod individuals within the stupor of their "blasé attitude."
This phrase is Georg Simmel's, referring to a condition that
arises from the constant jostling of the urban experience.[19]
It is a sickness in which the over-stimulated seek further
stimulation. Shock becomes, in the words of the theorist
Homer Simpson, "the cause of and solution to" our
predicament.[20] In *Parrot and Olivier in America,* Peter Carey
captures beautifully the rituals of these "agitated" moderns,
in his narrator's mock horror of a rocking chair. Razzed
by the social and financial mobilities of democracy, they
can not sit still. Instead, they must calm themselves via
neurotic repetition: motion that simulates movement.[21]
For its critics, this society produces a strain of traumatic
automatism that recalls Adorno's distaste for "pop" records
on endless repeat.

Perhaps for this reason, contemporary forms
of horror remain fated to a state of adolescence. They
appear evacuated of meaningful content, and can only
be rehabilitated through the admission of their triviality.
When employed for "serious" art, or for credible culture—
as in the films of Andy Warhol, Lars von Trier and Quentin
Tarantino, or in Francis Ford Coppola's remake of *Dracula*—
horror is reborn as camp. This is understandable. In its
realism, its need to communicate, horror necessarily flirts
with the literalness of kitsch. This is less a concern of more

abstract arts, if we believe Gillo Dorfles' claim that bad taste grows from representation.[22] Perhaps this vulgar tendency leads to the exile of horror into the spheres of "freak chic," either in dodgy cinemas or in museums. It remains with us, a kind of fellow traveler. But horror appears here not as its own, theorized entity. Instead it is a kind of spectral eminence, enmeshed in the strategies of contemporary art. This occurs in the operations of Kurt Schwitters, alongside other Modernists who attempted to express the jolting nature of their historical moment. The sublime goes "underground," only to reappear as Vito Acconci, audibly masturbating beneath the floor of a gallery.[23]

In this role, horror dramatizes the failure of abstraction. It involves "graphic" violence, and gruesome effects. There is a physicality in these, an insistence on the bodily. While the uncanny may be highly abstract—a vaporous or creeping unease—modern horror is more commonly awfully literal. There are ghosts and specters, in Rudyard Kipling's stories for example, which instill in their victims a kind of purified melancholic sensation. This is absolutely uncanny, but it does not evoke true horror.[24] The ghost is a "floating signifier;" it usually *denotes* a horror, a "murther most foul." The uncanny signals that something unnatural has occurred. Horror shows it to you, in gory detail.[25]

The artist Paul Thek often exploited this juxta-position, staging contrasts between the abstractions of art and latex casts resembling pieces of meat and bone. Thek famously "re-re-appropriated" the icons of Warhol, and combined them with his simulated butcher-shop cuttings. In the most sly example, a Brillo box is shown upturned, with a kind of spinal flap in its hollow underbelly.[26] Thek asserted the very explicit, literal fleshliness lurking in the body of twee works of minimalism and Pop. His gruesome container forces together two violently opposed modes of representation. It makes use of a bogus realism—gore as it would be modeled by a special effects studio—which intrudes into the rarefied atmosphere of commercial iconography and its seizure by sophisticated art.

The staging of horror, its social scandal, frequently operates through this type of assertion. Think, for example, of the Sex Pistols: their threatening and incomprehensible physicality, which was ritualized through sputum, vomit, blood, piercings, and "senseless" acts of violence. Again, the mounting abstraction of the pop product, its fetishistic resolution into a "thing," was resisted through a kind of tactical incontinence.[27] This failure of abstraction was likewise a horrifying effect of 9/11, in which the envelope of multi-national capital was peeled to disgorge its contents. The aerie of finance was opened, and what fell out were not equations but a cascade of paper, dust, metal, plastic, and other. Although ideologically opposed, the aesthetic strategies of Lydon and Laden were, at root, perhaps not so different.

Thek's horrors echo in the output of some contemporary British artists, who also fill the interior of abstract containers with blood and guts. This is clearly the case in Damien Hirst's installations of rotting or cross-sectioned creatures, which occupy technical chambers that look like Mies van der Rohe's Farnsworth House. These are flooded with formaldehyde or fetid air, providing a life-support system that also clearly plays a rhetorical role as foil to the gore—as with Marc Quinn's famous bust crafted of his own blood, preserved in a glass fridge. But even here,

1. Paul Thek, *Meat Piece with Warhol Brillo* Box, 1965 from the series *Technological Reliquaries*; wax, painted wood and Plexiglas, 35.6 x 43.2 x 43.2 cm, Philadelphia Museum of Art

1

2

3

2. John Isaacs, *Let The Golden Age Begin*, 2004, wax, polyester, paint, 70 x 70 x 70 cm   3. John Isaacs, *Everyone's Talking About Jesus*, 2005, wax, epoxy resin, polystyrene, 200 x 150 x 150 cm

questions remain as to whether the atmosphere of horror devalues the work. The products of the "YBAs" have often been dismissed as expensive shock-tricks, juvenilia lacking a more subtle imagination. Even Hirst himself claimed, probably disingenuously, that the shark in the tank was unnecessary to its sublime effect; the formaldehyde should have been enough.[28]

Despite their passage through the "correct" channels—such as Goldsmith's—these celebrated objects quite closely resemble others which are obviously in questionable taste. It did not go unnoticed when their ur-patron, Charles Saatchi, purchased the defunct Hammer horror film studio in 1997. Hirst's work, certainly, often appears as a conceptually over-freighted (and rather more technically crude) analogue of Gunther von Hagens' *Body Worlds* expositions. In some instances, the methods of the two are closely resembling. The German anatomist, for example, also cuts his "plastinated" remains into thin layers. Von Hagens' sections are delicate, but the atmosphere of horror is perhaps even more powerfully felt.

This has to do, in part, with the way that von Hagens handles his subject matter. *Body Worlds* is not just slightly literal. It is crushingly, pornographically literal—closely resembling the way that "adult" media approaches the irreducibility of its object.[29] In porn, technical means appear to bring the viewer ever closer to sexual pleasure. This fails, of course, resulting in a *danse macabre* of Adornian repetition: the venereal equivalent of the rocking chair. It is reproduction in the age of mechanical reproduction. *Body Worlds* maintains a similarly problematic relationship to its own object: life. The eye penetrates ever further, but ultimately fails to understand anything about the animating force of human existence. The person appears as a shocking marionette, an exchange of hydraulic and mechanical armatures for movement, and little else.

Sublime horror is alive and well, here. Von Hagens does not surrender his claim upon didactic objectives, despite his being criticized for pandering to prurient interest. In Romantic tradition, the shock encounter with death is intended to be instructive, to speak to the question of what is human. This is attempted *through the literal*, in the presentation of the material itself as a form of horrifying evidence. Again this mirrors pornography. There is no meaningful information, just an efflorescence of circumstantial detail. What you get in both cases is meat, a sort of corporeal poverty. "Bare life." Due to the taxidermist's brio, the meat can be chopped, sliced, unfolded, and flayed. But it cannot be abstracted; the presentation is utterly literal, comprising nothing but the artifact itself. While some "plastid" installations show their objects in isolation—they are removed from system or context and thus take on the false semblance of generality—no other medium is employed in the service of explanation. Von Hagen's work grows more from the cultural obsession with forensics as a mode of representation, in which the gore, itself, is made to speak.

So, where does this leave us? The final stop in this historical trajectory, from the sublime to the ridiculous, is the so-called "horror film." But even here, in its most apparently debased guise, there remains an unsettling power. This power is diametrically opposed to that claimed for the horrible by Kant or von Hagens: the affective shortcut to truth. By contrast, the ultimate message of the "fright flick" seems to be a profound commitment to indeterminacy. We

can see this clearly in the contrast with detective films. As literary critic Franco Moretti tells us, the gumshoe-and-cop shows are all about restoration. The world is disordered and then put to rights. Despite their carnivalesque atmosphere of social transgression, these works are driven by a conservative impulse. The message of such fiction is that there is a force, amoral or peri-criminal though its motivations may be, which does the work of knowledge: killers are found, reasons are unearthed. We, the moral public, find out whodunit and whydoit. If Moretti is to be believed, these works are modernist and epistemological: in short, they *assert the possibility of knowing*.[30]

Horror films brook no such positivism. Their outcome tends to be morally ambiguous and inconclusive at best. After all, the great cliché of the genre is the killer or monster rising from the grave for one last tweak before the credits roll. The message is: this will all begin again, see you soon. The import of modern horror is perpetual derangement, and this is why—in addition to their performance as commodities—a "franchise" always seems to produce endless sequels. There is no search for truth through shock, and no will to our moral restitution. The "we" of horror is a sort of lunatic fringe, the trench coat crowd, who identify with violence as a way of letting their

The typical shock ending of the horror film

freak flag fly. This may be a kind of directionless, dystopic melancholy, as with the teenage goths and Black Metal fans. It may be genuine sociopathology of one form or another. Or, more commonly, it could be a kind of tourism which allows normal folks to slum it on the dark side for a couple of hours.

The truth is probably a combination of these, and also likely depends on the product itself. The sinister fringe (and teenagers) are probably served by the genre of "torture porn:" films such as *Hostel* (2005), the *Saw* series (2004-present), or *The Human Centipede* (2010). However, box office receipts would attest to the popularity of films that adapt this seedy repertoire to more complex ends, such as David Fincher's *Seven* (1995), Tarantino's *Kill Bill* (2003-4), or the Stieg Larssen novels and their adaptations. In this context, at least, horror has thus become something of a "kick," not serious social inquiry or aesthetic investigation. This would be the case even with respect to films such as the *Day Of The Dead* (1985), which smuggle arch commentary beneath the splatter. These are interesting, but they hardly support the high-flown claims made for horror in past centuries.

Is horror still relevant, then? More than ever. If we believe Naomi Klein, it has emerged, in the guise of "shock," as the central force in a new economic, political, and cultural order. In this form, a sounding of the soul functions in the service of intimidation and pacification. It becomes, in effct, a weapon of social control. Its use gives rise to a collectively sanctioned state of emergency or sovereign "exception," in which centralized authority can be expanded in the name of order. The continual threat of de-stabilization, of chaos and anarchy, justifies the incremental seizures of the public sphere by capital and its official facilitators.[31] The excesses of the second Bush presidency are, perhaps, the most convincing evidence put forward for this theory.

In this politics of the sublime, horror has been matched by Terror. In many ways, the imagery of 9/11 represented the absolute apex of the picturesque—condensing the sublimity of height and speed with the epochal imagery of fallen civilizations, the hubris of Babel, Oriental siege, Rome burning, acts of god, birds alighting moments before the impact, and so forth. Cameras showed Turner clouds, like a new Krakatoa, rising vortiform to block out the sun. The photographs of Ground Zero, showing fragments of the towers' facades, looked like a hypertrophied Tintern Abbey. Terror is not art, but it is certainly an aesthetic proposition. It transmits a Burkean experience, a messianic and transformative violence, but its charisma is quickly institutionalized. True to Burke's ideas, this is a *sondage* with a strongly conservative backdraft. The powers that be quickly converted the post-9/11 moment into a state of heightened social quiescence, a fearful consensus.

There is, also, a more general "rediscovery" of affect underway. This asserts itself through a variety of manifestations: from charismatic religion, to academic theory appealing to emotion, to "experiential environments" and material effects that would add sensational optics to the products of the architect. Such emphases suggest the extent to which the Enlightenment project of knowing has fallen into a moment of crisis.[32] At the least, it is losing influence to a neo-Romanticism in which *feeling is believing*.

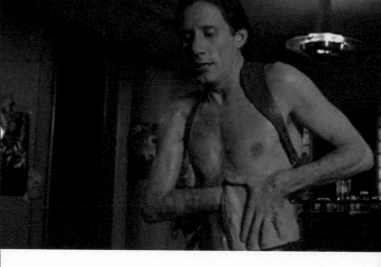

Against this backdrop, the historical attraction of horrors is their assumed purchase on the soul. After all, their sublimity has long been thought to congeal, to *realize*, those things out of reach: the spirit, natural laws and essences, authentic divinity and human dignity, among others.

But this is not the whole story. As we will see, horror also reorients one to the notion that what exists is not necessarily all that might be. It is a very vulgar form of materialism, to be sure, but—like those slasher films—one with counterintuitive consequences. As in Paul Thek's art, there is a moment in which horror becomes the basis for a failure in the stability of objects, in the very "thingness" of things. And this is where we begin to engage the enticing problem of deviance.

A videocasette slot in James Woods' abdomen, Videodrome, 1983

Deviant Anatomy

Against this history, we will look at bodily horrors and their analogues in the built environment. These are instances in which normal anatomy grows deviant—extra limbs appear, holes open where they should not, individuals are doubled and split and copied. In such discomfiting operations, we limn the rise of an "anti-ontology," a kind of multi-focal, multiply-inhabited way of being.

This follows classic tropes of abomination, monstrous forms reaching back to Rabelais and before: mismatched limbs and morphemes; transgressions of the line between natural and non-; elements out-of-place; crossed borders and cultures, inappropriate intimacies.[33] In these wretched examples, the boundary between subject and world, self and other, does not coincide with the limits of the body. Rather, they may include foreign objects, as in *Pantagruel*'s image of the drunk intersected with his barrel. Or they are horribly incontinent, with restless pieces that invade their neighbors in the crepuscular hours.[34] These can appear unnatural, or ugly. But they are also creative and exceedingly energetic.

These, too, have been imagined differently at various moments. Curiously, aberration and "monstrous" exception have not always implied evil or ugliness. As Hillel Schwartz quotes Montaigne:

> What we call monsters are not so to God, who sees in the immensity of His work the infinity of forms that He has comprised...there is nothing that is contrary to nature.[35]

There are those who have seen those things internally heterogeneous as a sort of divine emergence, the upwelling of new design—who have not mistaken convention for beauty, and vice versa. Schwartz, for one, notes the changing interpretation of the monster from a "marvel, an amazing *thing* under God's heaven," to the "monster as multiplicity, a polyform *being* nursed by extravagant Nature."[36] Likewise, the poet Gerard Manley Hopkins wrote in "Pied Beauty" of the blessed character

Tricephalous Christ, Salisbury Cathedral

of the polyglot. Like Montaigne, and later Jacques Derrida, Hopkins credited God with "dappled things," for all "counter, original, spare, strange." Kant, similarly, claimed that "multiplicity is beauty."[37] The unique and the multiform merely show the breadth of the Lord's creation.

While it has not been simply equated with ugliness or perversity, deviant anatomy has usually signaled the presence of the exceptional. The notion of physical aberration has often been associated with figures of power, with kings and deities. Horrid forms were often used to conceptualize superhuman sovereignty. In the Medieval church, for example, some morphological experiments were even applied to the godhead. Prior to the resolution of Jesus' familiar image, artists tried to tackle the problem of the Trinity: a god that was simultaneously three and one. This resulted in the Tricephalous Christ: a three-headed figure, intersected at the cheek.[38] This was used briefly before being declared *anathema*. Celtic Christianity was likewise subject to odd formal compromises, centuries of secret accommodation with Druidic and "folk" religions.[39] One example was the Anglo-Saxon crucifixion: Jesus and King Arthur, intersected with a tree. Here, brambles replace the cross; tangled branches pierce the flesh like nails.[40]

As with the superhuman, the anomalous body has provided a medium for pondering the boundaries of the species, and those of the individual subject. This frequently has to do with the horizon of humanity, blurring the demarcation between animals and ourselves. This is, of course, a classic of carnival: bestial masks and behaviors, creatures dignified with human titles and honorifics, dogs walking on their hind legs. The mythical spawn of classical antiquity—fawns, minotaurs, lycanthropes, nymphs and

sylphs—very commonly straddled this uneasy interface. Others combined different animals into a single being, or multiples of the same in a conjoined body, like Cerberus.

This last, when applied to the human, provides another major strain of horror. The European folk traditions include a large number of many-headed giants and ogres, multiple selves forced into the unbearable intimacy of a single body, with shared hungers and movements, hearts and assholes. The nightmare of the partial individual, who must share core elements of his subjectivity with others, is a gross contravention of the territorial anatomy—at least in those cultures where liberal humanism was on the ascent.

The deviant, then, might be called a type of "experimental subject," a mode of being that articulates human experience under shifting circumstances. The mania would be particularly acute when the pace of history, for whatever reason, appears to us as abnormally brisk. No coincidence, perhaps, were those outbreaks of freaks in the so-called Age of Revolutions, among the Victorians, or

The Bunker Family

more recently in an era of "trans-localization," when the geographies of wealth and connection come to seem ever more opaque and conspiratorial.

As Franco Moretti observed, the two archetypal Modern monsters—he with the electrodes, and he with the pointy teeth—emerge as the "horrible faces of a single society, its *extremes*: the disfigured drone and the ruthless proprietor."[41] That is, labor and capital in an early modern moment. Frankenstein shows man penetrated and demolished by technology, forced to perform a kind of St. Vitus' Dance on the factory floor, cadaverous and automated. By contrast, Dracula is the ur-exploiter depicted by Marxian theory, a sort of deified junkie: both the beneficiary, and victim, of capital. His amazing powers of extraction become a form of enslavement. Both figures embody a fear of what is to come: "[expressing] the anxiety that the future will be monstrous."[42]

In a similar manner, the "Siamese" twins known as Chang and Eng gave embodiment to fear and ambivalence surrounding the threat of civil war to the "curious institution" of the antebellum South. This was due to the fact that the famous brothers—having taken the surname Bunker and married two portly American sisters—settled in North Carolina's Blue Ridge Mountains and accumulated a double-homestead comprising twenty-two children and over thirty slaves. When P.T. Barnum offered to pay for their separation in 1868, many writers (Mark Twain among them) saw this as a ripe metaphor for the tenuous state of the nation. Would the twins be separated, or "would the union be preserved?"[43]

In making problematic the boundaries of the human actor, the aberration raises questions about the

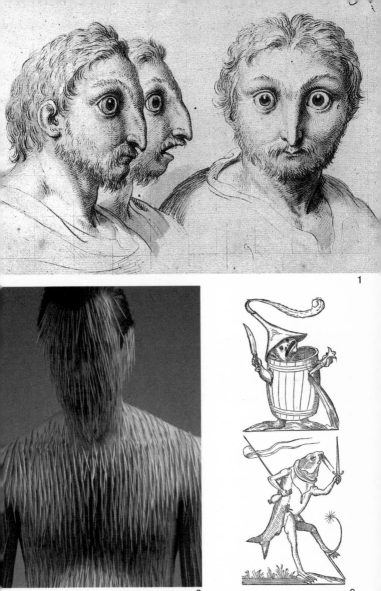

1. Charles LeBrun, *Men-Hoot-Owls*, 1671 2. Lucy McRae,
Pic of Sticks, 2009 3. Rabelais' *Pantagruel and Gargantua*

shifting contradictions of social context. He embodies the Freudian uncanny: alien yet uncomfortably near, ourselves in the form of the other. As Moretti writes, the monster "serves to displace the antagonisms and horrors evidenced *within* society *outside* society itself."[44] Here it stands objectified, as with the case of Shelley's and Stoker's symbols of exploitation, or in the figure of the cannibal who frequently appears in the pop-mythology of the Chinese Cultural Revolution and more recently in the writing of Mo Yan.[45] But this is merely one historical theme among many. Wherever there appears a perceived erosion of the conventions and structures that hold the seams (and the semes) together, monsters begin to emerge.

The horrible has thus to do, in part, with a shifting of territorial borders. This is true of bodies; it is also true of geographies. It moves the line of radical alterity, that which separates ourselves and others, to an inappropriate location. The seam or suture represents a joining of the unlike. The migration of borders often creates a misalignment between historically established communities and their spaces, as in states born of imperial fiat. Such is the case, today, with the flows of the trans-local. As with Achille Mbembe's account of Africa, the manifold products of the *entrepôt* and the "global city" unfold under the sign of the horrid, their very being demonstrating a secret history of "strange signs," "convulsive movments," and "monstrous couplings."[46]

The abnormality thus gives imaginative form to anxieties about being human under evolving conditions, in a de-familiarized world. Horror is a notion that embodies both intimacy and "blasphemous alienage,"[47] figuring the plight of modern subjects "at two with nature," with our circumstances, and with our selves.

Horror in Architecture

"You have always been a frightful mirror, a monstrous instrument of repetitions…"
Julio Cortázar[48]

This immanence of horror in the dynamism of the modern is nowhere clearer than in architecture. As elsewhere, built horrors have an intimate connection to the birth and death of historical forms. Many will remember Walter Benjamin's famous dictum that each great work signals the arrival of a new genre. This is heroic nonsense. New types—whether literary or architectural—are, in fact, born long before they are recognized. These are often greeted not as advancements but as oddities. Their arrival appears abominable: a mother birthing the child of a different species. This problematical nativity is often due to an historical process, such as a shift in the dominant "mode of production."[49] Various socio-economic orders have hatched the tragedy, the comedy, the essay, and the novel, after their own image. Each has been retroactively hailed as an authentic expression of its time. Regardless, their morphogenesis was initially thought freakish. Herein the real avant-garde: awkward amalgams and provisional gestures.

Even "canonical" works have been viewed, in their infancy, as dubious. For this reason Michel de Montaigne, while producing an influential mode of philosophical writing, labeled his own essays "monstrous bodies, pieced together of diverse members, without definite shape, having no order, sequence, or proportion other than accidental."[50]

Likewise, we might understand Henry James' acid dismissal of the Russian novel as a "loose, baggy, monster." A similar charge has been leveled at the work of James Joyce, at Jean Genet's autobiographical writing, and also at some of Jacques Derrida's philosophical experiments.[51] In particular, formal innovators—modern bricoleurs foremost among them—have been cast as Frankensteinian: those who would cobble unseemly bodies from available fragments.

In architecture, the horrible frequently appears at the historical interface of language and type. In such a moment, the resources of an existing vocabulary are put under pressure by changes in scale or composition, required by accelerated socio-economic development. The transitional building appears ill-formed, as its devices are maladapted to its task. The good old tricks no longer work. The architect is forced to deploy his conventions in ungrammatical assemblages, as a new language has not yet arisen that is capable of solving the aesthetic problem of the new type. That is to say: the horrid wells up when the techniques of one historical moment are applied to the needs of another.

So what does such a building look like? One can see this, for example, in the architecture of the so-called American Commercial Renaissance (approx. 1840-1929). Many of the first great palaces of trade—mushrooming arcades and office towers—rose during this period to meet the practical needs of the new industrial class, as well as to express the self-image of American financial power.[52] New orders of retail and recreational space came to prominence in burgeoning urban areas: department stores, auditoria, and museums. These were of unprecedented size, sprawl and height.

The resulting aesthetic—one of "crowding," is seen throughout much urban American architecture of the period. But it is also seen elsewhere, in the new press of humanity around the *locus horribilus* of the commercial. As E.L. Doctorow later described it, in *Ragtime*, "there seemed to be no entertainment that did not involve great swarms of people."[53] In essence, the social problem of the age was one of unprecedented numbers, sizes, and densities; in architecture and wherever the moderns gathered. As such, the regnant language of Neoclassicism collided violently with the hyperbolic proportions of the modern. The accommodation of architecture to new problems of scale and scope required prolonged experimentation and produced many rank failures; a menagerie of suggestive creatures sprang up along the way.

Architects of the period experimented wildly with the application of historical styles and compositional tricks to this problem. While a stubborn conundrum, the large and complex structure nonetheless created opportunities for innovation. This was particularly true of the tower. Raymond Hood, designer of many significant examples, "felt that the skyscraper problem was still a relatively new phenomenon in American architecture, lacking any established traditions or strict formulas." Hood, for one, "was quite happy with the prevailing mood in which everyone could try out whatever idea came into their head."[54] This was likewise the case with other emergent typologies.

Take, for example, the Grandstand of the thoroughbred racetrack at Washington Park, Chicago (1884). The latter illustrates precisely that moment in which a fundamentally new challenge faces vernacular conventions. This question is quite straightforward: how does one design a very large building? The answer is far from clear. Huge surfaces and volumes test the ability of the architect to create a coherent, harmonious composition. Should one dispose of the great expanses of the modern building by adding more elements—that is, by increasing their number—or by making each larger?

In order to tackle the dilemma of scale, Solon S. Beman chose to replicate the configuration of a normal construction. He did so by scaling everything up, by enlarging all constituent pieces proportionally. Beman attempted to solve the problem of the large building by applying to it the familiar composition of something much smaller. In fact, the Grandstand is not a great edifice, so much as it is a modest one inflated. Its massing and disposition of parts clearly suggests a more diminutive object. Beman's work mimics the architecture of a suburban retreat; it recalls the Evanston Country Club and the Glen View Club, both by Holabird and Roche, or the Shinnecock Hills Golf Clubhouse, in Long Island, by McKim, Mead and White.[55]

In order to maintain this illusion, all the ingredients of a pitched roof were up-sized simultaneously; turrets, chimneys, and gables all acquired extraordinary dimensions so as to appear visually consonant with one another. The illusion might have worked, perhaps, if one were to see the stands unoccupied. The image is alarming precisely because it is inhabited; the expanse of Beman's super-roof is read against the crowd beneath. With visitors on the verandas, the Grandstand looks like the product of trick photography, some clever photo-montage in which it has been populated by Lilliputians. The fact that one can

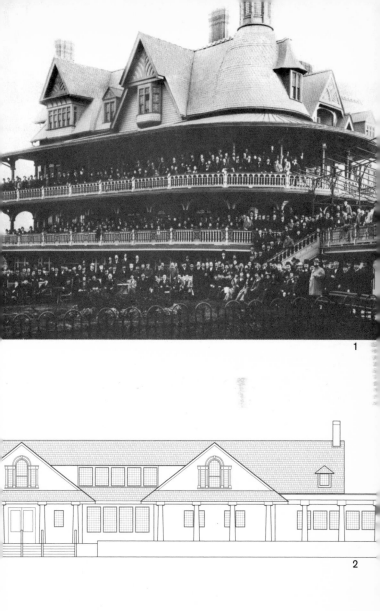

1. Solon S. Beman, Grandstand at Washington Park, Chicago   2. McKim, Mead, and White, Shinnecock Hills Golf Clubhouse, Long Island, New York

read the massive gables against the human form contributes to the impression of the roof as a great looming behemoth. It looks as if Piranesi designed a country club.

The illusion of a giant roof, and the artifice employed in its production, suggests an architectural folly. It is a kind of "special effect" used in circumstances where the normal rules do not apply: in whimsical garden pavilions, pleasure palaces, Vegas and the Vatican. An example of this is Bernard Maybeck's Palace of Fine Arts, in which the great vaults structure a mammoth scenography of ruin. Beman's grandstand also recalls the work of Postmodernists such as Michael Graves and Robert A.M. Stern, who employed intentionally mis-scaled components. Likewise, it resembles a strain of rhetorical building in which a single over sized element is made to stand metonymically for the whole, as in Adolf Loos' entry to the *Chicago Tribune* Tower competition, or in the *architectures parlantes* of Boullée and LeDoux. True to the tradition of deviant anatomy, the Grandstand's unique scalar expression creates a formal instability. It appears to be two things at once: a new typology which occupies (problematically) the skin of its forebear.

This method is by no means an obvious choice. Other architects of Beman's time assayed the problem of the large building in rather different ways. While some likewise relied upon over scaling, others chose the path of repetition: that is, of incorporating elements of more conventional size, but in greater number. Others merged both techniques into yet more complex hybrids.

Beman's odd result was not due to lack of inventiveness or skill. The repertoire of the Neoclassical building was simply ill-equipped to deal with the engorged bulk of the modern. The Victorian architect produced his work within a language dedicated to the articulation of specificity. In the lingering pre-modern vocabulary, exceptions were the dominant object of architectural attention. Ornamentation was used to heighten particular conditions, exceptional moments within the tectonic of a building: frames surrounding openings and edges, coursing defining the line between floors, columns visualizing lines of vertical force, etcetera.

This language combined none too easily with a nascent architecture of repetition, system, and number. This did not merely have to do with questions of scale. The techniques of the pre-20th-century designer were likewise strained by the tendency of the modern building to move away from the singular and the exceptional, in favour of the aesthetics of mass quantity. In this moment of expansion, elements such as enframed windows—those last vestiges of the individual in architecture—continued to be used, and were subject to a disturbing proliferation.

This effect is visible in another of Solon S. Beman's works, the Pullman Building. This example contrasts his Grandstand. At Pullman, the ornamentation of the windows—their celebration as "events" in the façade—disagrees with their proliferation. The result reminds one of a creature with too many of something; a swarm of eyes, perhaps. The sheer number of elements seems yet more absurd when each is "heightened" by the use of decorative treatments. Likewise, the corona of chimneys, domes, and turrets appears inappropriate and excessive. These are of conventional size, and a huge building such as Pullmann requires them to be used in far greater numbers. The result is an expression of immoderate surplus.

Solon S. Beman, Pullman Building, Chicago

The manic repetition of bits, each articulated as a feature, makes for a particular variety of strangeness. En masse, these contribute to an "aesthetics of crowding:" a sort of liberal nightmare in which the individual unit cannot be properly assimilated into the expression of a collective. The Pullman is a monster after the Leviathan, at least after the famous engraving on the title page of Thomas Hobbes' book.[56] It appears a meld of independent entities that have not been, or cannot be, assimilated into the morphology of a greater corporate body. There remains an unresolved tension between the whole and its parts. Hence we might understand many of the awkward products of late Victoriana, their tremulous density and corseted appearance—as if they were barely restraining a bolus of forces.

In such examples, one can oppose the disturbing form of the early modern building with the cool towers of Mies van der Rohe that were later to come to the Loop.[57] Mies' works solve the problems of size and repetition by assimilating everything into an aesthetics of system. Herein, all components of the façade are subsumed within the expression of the grid. The Miesian building signals the historical retreat of specificity into pattern. At Seagram's, the lines of the window extend vertically and horizontally to the edge of the façade; the window thus appears merely as an interpolation of continuous horizontal and vertical lines.[58] The modernist resolution was to express the frame itself as primary organizational device.[59] As opposed to the weak classicism of Beman and Jenney, the Miesian system is infinite. Like grids and patterns in general, the surface of buildings such as 860-880 Lake Shore Drive could go on indefinitely. Their limits appear purely arbitrary.

By contrast, early high-rises had a problematic multiplicity, a kind of schizoid or doubly-inhabited form. Still today, they present an anachronism. In scalar terms they are modern, in language they are Neoclassical, "Saracenic," Gothic, or Romanesque.

The enlargement and involution of buildings shadowed an analogous trend in the evolution of commercial institutions more generally. The period that gave rise to the pleasing horrors of the Chicago Loop was noted for its burgeoning monopolies. Businesses and production chains—like buildings—became ever more vertically integrated. That strange goliath, the corporation, emerged. This same economic logic that birthed department stores such as Marshall Field's, in which the main street of yesteryear was internalized. As Lewis Mumford argued in 1961, the "combination of...expansion and congestion, horizontal and vertical, [produce] the maximum opportunities for profit."[60] The architectural consequences remain profound.

Consolidation and enlargement exert their influence in the production of a variety of horrible architectures. As do other uniquely modern forces, which we will discuss in what follows: mass repetition of buildings and components, expansions in the structural possibilities of their height and span, new technologies and social practices, the restless re-valuations of urban real estate, and the global transmission of architectural iconography.

This is not merely the quandary of a certain moment of American architectural history. Quite the contrary. Horror is ever emergent. It reasserts itself whenever the established language of building is overtaken by the historical rate of change, and by the consequent

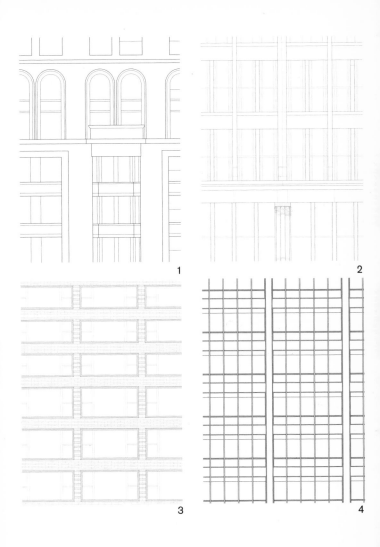

1. Holabird and Roche, Marquette Building, Chicago   2. Jenney and Mundie, Leiter Building, Chicago   3. Louis Sullivan, Carson Pirie Scott, Chicago   4. Mies van der Rohe, 800-860 Lake Shore Drive, Chicago

1. Entries to the Chicago Tribune Tower Competition by William
Eugene Drummond (left), John Mead Howells and Raymond Hood
2. Holabird and Roche, Hotel Muehlebach, Kansas City, Missouri

requirements of new typologies. It is a chronic symptom of modernity's violent and cyclical dynamism, its expansions and convulsions and metamorphoses. For this reason, unease remains endemic in the built environment.

We might see this, for example, in the case of more recent inventions, such as the shopping mall and the "expo center." The difficulty of these horrid objects is well known: they are simply too big to be given any kind of uniform identity. Many are even too large for the expansive abstractions of modern architecture, and their design has (by necessity) tended to favor the episodic and the fragmented. Its contents are understood myopically, as merely a jumble of retail environments or "experiential spaces," each as small as a single perceptible envelope.

Whereas the Miesian building attempted to drown the horror of the modern scale in the cool liquidity of abstraction, the gawky "transitional" building—either of the Chicago loop or of the contemporary megastructural economy—exposes intransigent questions of outsized architecture. Where the Modernists surrender to the infinite, to Kant's mathematical sublimity, the 19th-century architect tried desperately to domesticate size through the ornamental treatment of edges, levels, and openings. Similarly, today's designer tries to refract it into a welter of micro-environments. By doing so, they expose an unsettling presence that only appeared to disappear, by sleight of hand, in the fleeting elegance of Modernist technique.

The Redemption of Horror

How can horror be situated in a contemporary enterprise of reading and making architecture?

We have claimed that horror continues to stalk our physical environment, as well as its aesthetic and artistic theorization—that it is immanent in the modern, and problematically so. It must be sublimated through design, or taken up in the work of a "negative" avant-garde: a history of post-humanist or dystopian projects that link Hirst to Hilberseimer to Himmelblau.[61]

Horror is the leitmotif of an architecture forced to continually transform; an architecture that, in this process, appears beleagured by, and ambivalent about, aesthetics. At least, in their traditional, "compositional" guise. Emergent architecture, circa now, trends more toward affect and effect, toward modes of systematized sublimity that include the mass movement of particles (mobilized through parametrics), the improbable variety, or the looming cantilever. These are the built analogue of a broader epistemic crisis, in which evocations of sensation—the ecstatic, the charismatic, the pornographic and the revolting—are the medium of a new artistic and political order. Here, again, they are matched by the politics of "shock," and of a trend toward the affective in the arts, in the academic, and in popular culture. The sublime is on the march, again.

But architectural horrors do not sit easily with this trend, in any simple sense. They are *in* the moment, but not *of* it. Horror is also paradoxically uneasy with respect to contemporary architecture, with its patterns, parameters, and diagrammatic postures. The inheritance of sublime terror is not nearly so elating, nor so beautifully aloof. Horror is one byproduct of the modern, and thus shares many of characteristics of its advanced forms, evolving with them. But at the same time, it remains a dark mirror, an unsettling or ungrateful fellow traveler—like all reflections, it remains opposed, while sharing many important formal characteristics. We will see many examples of this in what follows. These emerge from the logic of their time, but often appear inverted and unsettling, a counter-discourse stretching from the Romantic to the parametric. They are, again, both intimate and alien.

For this reason, we can look at horrors to find architectural alternatives. At them, and through them. We do so because they reveal blind spots, cataracts—things that we are not properly supposed to find. Openings dwell at the limit of the thinkable, at the edge of the epistemic spotlight, *even though they are right in front of our faces*. In this, horrors offer a lens; no more, no less.

The point of architectural horrors is not that they necessarily revolt or mortify. This would overstate their emotive impact. They rarely harrow our souls, so much as they present a discomfiting image of mutation and change. Some are genuinely frightening—such as Vietnam's Hang Na Villa. Yves Marchand and Romain Meffre's images of Detroit buildings, partially and mostly dead, are chilling for their distorted appearance as well as their social implications. Others, such as South China Mall, are worrying and amusing at the same time. In what follows, we present a large number of examples, past and present, disturbing and lovely, doltish and sophisticated (or both). In true 18th-century style, we choose to divorce these from boring and unhelpful judgments about their beauty or ugliness. Some of these are ugly, to be sure. Others are achingly beautiful. But more importantly, all present the possibilities of deviant architecture as an opening into new worlds of form, composition, space-making, program, and hierarchy.[62]

Let's not react to this hysterically. Here, "horrors" refers to peculiar buildings or urbanisms, that can be read through biophysical analogues or creatures from popular history. We divide these into general tropes, points on a spectrum of morphological deviance. These contain varied elements of the "horrible," such as doubling, reiteration, disproportion, formlessness, shifts of scale, excess parts or openings, solidity, and the like. This does not imply that such works are necessarily appalling or negative, although some certainly are. The buildings in this book are selected simply because they are interesting—because *they say something important about what architecture might be or become*.

When we look specifically at architectures, a new matrix of alterity emerges. Here, it is about artifice and mutability: about the deviation between "naturalized" norms and other, more rarefied, possibilities. Deviant buildings, as one would expect, represent conditions that reconfigure the conventions of the architectural object— substituting deformity for conformity. These mutations generalize quickly under pressure, staking a claim as the genomics of a new order. For example, we consider how the modernist assumption of the building as a single, coherent object has recently been inverted: fragmentation, a totally opposed compositional principle, is now *de rigeur*, in worlds of commercial expediency as well as elite cultural production. Here we might claim that an exception in architecture—what Maurice Blanchot called a "monstrous singularity"—can very quickly become the basis for a new kind of rule.[63]

Horror suggests a desire to understand and value deviance; to be suspicious of fundamentals and appearances; to let the norm be weirded by the exception. What follows, then, is a provocation—or a manual, or a guide, or an alternative canon. What it is depends on what one would do with it. Properly speaking, horror has no manifesto. It is not an "ism," and it is certainly not a school, a movement, or a cell. It is only a kind of tolerance, a willingness to look. It embodies the suspicion that official design discourses are not telling the whole story, and that spaces for action are to be found in an expanded aesthetic field—one that marries the beautiful to the distorted, the awkward, the manifold and the indeterminate.

Typologies Of Horror

Doubles and Clones

"Opposition is true Friendship."
William Blake[1]

We begin with a subject that is perhaps most basic to horror, and to the kindred subjects of the *unheimlich* and the monstrous: the failure of the body, and the person, as a unique or singular entity. In *The Uncanny*, doubling is said to be associated with "mirror-images, shadows, guardian spirits, the doctrine of the soul and fear of death."[2] For Freud, the *döppelganger* is repellent for invoking the animist practice in which an effigy, a mask or statue, would be forged as insurance against mortality. The duplicate was a form of decoy, a hiding place for the soul. In an argument that recalls Adorno's theory of ugliness, Freud described the *unheimlich* double as a hollowed vestige of this earlier custom. It impels the awareness of a "primitive phase" in our mental development when sympathetic magic—the power of resembling objects over one another—was believed to be effective. Certainly, the echo of these enchantments can be heard when the *döppelganger* appears in fiction, often as a hijacking of the true self. This is the case in Nikolai Gogol's "The Nose," when Major Kovalyov discovers that this organ has absconded with his job and his social life. Likewise, in Dostoyevsky's "The Double," the protagonist can recognize his ego in an alien body, as it approaches in a darkened street. The second self and the "nemesis" are coextensive, as in the classic dualism of Sherlock Holmes and Moriarty, or in Chuck Palahniuk's Tyler Durden.

More immediately, perhaps, the human duplicate presents an existential conundrum: *it is neither one nor many*. The "individual" remains our preferred vision of the subject, and we are comfortable with siblings who exist within an expected range of resemblance. But identical twins—alongside albinos, cripples, the blind or the mute—have often been considered a sinister omen or a contravention of nature's laws. The excessive identity of the identical, applied to people, appears to violate the norms of deviation within a fraternal series.

In formal terms, twins are defined by a surplus of symmetry. Through mirroring, their symmetry is itself symmetrical. As such, they embody a super-abundance of the "harmony" valued in classical thought. This excess gives rise to an odd phenomenon: horrible beauty. This emerges, in particular, when each twin is conventionally beautiful unto him or herself. There is a conflict between

John Carpenter, *The Thing*, 1982

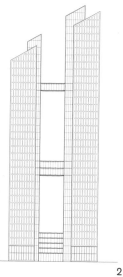

1. Sam Raimi, *Army of Darkness* 1992   2. Typical
semi-detached home   3. Highlight Tower, Munich

an apparently "ideal" object and its duplication. Whereas ugly twins are merely sad, lovely ones are alarming. This is the case with the Winklevoss brothers, both played by Armie Hammer in David Fincher's *The Social Network* (2010). In much the same way, Hugh Hefner's tendency to repeatedly squire identical sisters (and survive) smells like brimstone. Multiplication draws forward the threshold at which beauty gives way to discomfort. Oscar Wilde described such a reaction to Dorian Gray's unreal allure (again, produced by a duplication) which suggested inhuman artifice, and the corruption of other faculties. Wilde's horror of portraiture, of the occult sympathy between an object and its representation, is prescient with respect to photography, film, and the recorded voice— principal sites of the modern *unheimlich*.

Horrible beauty likewise operates in architecture, to various degrees. It was acute, for example, in the former towers of New York's World Trade Center. These differed from doubles such as the World Trade Center in Bahrain (2008), or the Cullinan in Hong Kong (2009). In the latter cases, the individual tower is asymmetrical; mirroring occurs at the scale of the pair. Similarly, instances such as the Highlight Towers in Munich (2004) appear as a single asymmetrical figure that has been bifurcated. By contrast, each of the two Manhattan skyscrapers gave the impression of being a perfection unto itself. Twinning— as opposed to mirroring—lent them a powerful symbolic aspect, as embodiments of "trade" and international capital. Each seemed ready to proliferate; nothing about their composition prevented the possibility of a third, or a fourth tower. The WTC appeared as merely one stage in an expansionary operation.

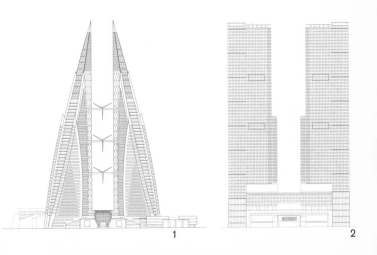

1. Bahrain World Trade Center   2. Cullinan, Hong Kong
3. Armie Hammer as Cameron and Tyler Winkelvoss

Subsequent twin-buildings have oscillated between the Scylla and Charybdis of unhappy outcomes: they are either boring for being repeated, or histrionic in their attempt to mitigate redundancy. The former category includes the breathtakingly unremarkable Time-Warner Center in Manhattan (2003); the Cullinan in Hong Kong (2009), which attempts to form a heroic gateway using the language of glass corporatism; or the Torres de Santa Cruz in Tenerife (2006). A contrasting anxiety is represented by the grotesque curves of Bahrain Financial Harbour (2009) or in the "techno sesame" aesthetic of that island kingdom's World Trade Centre.

Successful examples, such as Rafael Moneo's Kursaal in San Sebastian (1999) tend to avoid either tactic. Moneo's composition succeeds by skirting symmetry: the viewer feels continually on the verge of seeing the two theaters unfolding evenly to either side. This never happens, and the various imperfectly mirrored vistas offered by the building "in the round" are compelling. In this regard, it remembers Reima Pietilä's proposal for a multi-purpose center in Monte Carlo (1969), where a doubled mound withholds a symmetry anticipated from other angles. Such an effect can be directly contrasted, for example, with the Gate of Europe by Philip Johnson, in Madrid (1996). Here, the very sinister structural gimmick of the lean is exaggerated by crude mirroring. It is not surprising, perhaps, that this building was imagined as the *pied a terre* of Satan in the 1995 film *The Day of the Beast*.

In architecture, this problem of the double, a *folie a deux*, is yet stranger with physical attachment. This recalls conjoined or "Siamese" twins, the "shared body" typology of monsters such as Cerberus, and the tricephalous ogres

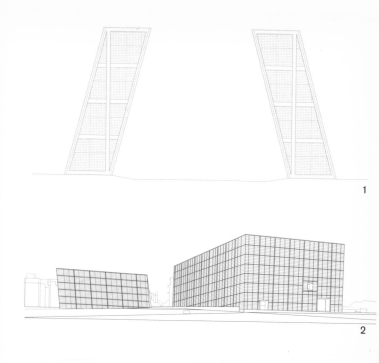

1

2

3

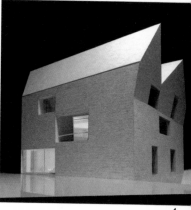

4

1. Philip Johnson, Gate of Europe, Madrid   2. Rafael Moneo, Kursaal, San Sebastian   3. Alejandro Aravena, Siamese Tower, Universidad Católica de Chile   4. Johnston Marklee, House House, Ordos, Inner Mongolia, PRC

in whom multiple creatures are biologically superimposed. Robert Mills, in his work on "Jesus as Monster," has argued that it is this conjoint doubling, the eclipse of the individual in one body, that is the most basic historical trope of monstrous aesthetics.[3] For modern humanism, this is a fundamental source of horror: the non-conformity of individual subject and unique body. Likewise, conjunction begins to distort symmetry, crimping elements as they approach the point of contact. Such anatomies commonly incorporate a lack or an "in-folding" of vestigial limbs that remain hidden within the body's recesses.

This discomfort reaches a kind of apex in the semi-detached house. The interest of the semi is due to the fact that this typology is always-already a deviant being, born of modern compromise: the oddly forced intimacy of the "two-family house." The dwelling looks bigger than it is, and lends an impression of upper-class gentility to an object defined by lower middle-class spatial possibilities. As such, it is reminiscent of those odd accommodations between politeness and economy to be found in the domestic circumstances of Balzac's characters, with all of their delicate nuances of commodity.[4] These might seem preferable to the crass repetition of the terrace or suburban subdivision (below). But while the latter appears uncannily de-personalized, it nonetheless avoids the press of two parties—dwelling instead in the modern anonymity of the masses.[5]

The prototypical form of these demi-houses suggests a failure to osmose. "Semi-detached" is a funny negative. It implies a sort of inability to achieve, completely, the status of the individual—to free oneself from social dependencies. Houses, we would believe, strive toward a moment of disengagement; semis remain trapped within the entanglements of a socio-typical privation. By the norms of bourgeois aspiration, they are "halfway" homes.

The clarity of juxtaposition between two halves of a semi begs them to be compared. Their duality suggests a dichotomy, of contrary or opposed natures. Following Jacob and Esau, we expect to see contrasts of noble and craven, conservative and progressive, pugnacious and affable. As Melville put it,

> Now envy and antipathy, passions
> irreconcilable in reason, nevertheless in fact
> may spring conjoined like Chang and Eng
> in one birth. Is Envy then such a monster?[6]

It is a common assumption that twins represent alternate poles of the human character. From Medea to Jekyll, to the contemporary heirs of Anthony Perkin's iconic psychopath, duality is assumed to involve a Manichean struggle between good and evil, normality and aberration. It is unsurprising, then, that these dualities would come to be projected upon the two halves of a shared house.

In former British colonies such as Australia and Singapore, the semi-detached house is a special site of horrid interaction. In many cases, owners on either side exercise their right to self-expression without concern for their neighbor. The result is a kind of mirroring, albeit freakish and inventive. Anything can be placed along the horizon between the two halves: Classicism meets Mediterranean, Modernism encounters Asian Village Baroque.

The inherently problematical nature of the semi is exacerbated in this context by a tendency to insist upon difference—the "warring" nature of the conjoined twins, in contrast to the anodyne image of the European or Canadian prototype. The British version articulates a desire to disappear into the larger social order, to dissolve with dignity. Not so the Singapore semi-dweller, for example, who does not retreat in such pacific fashion. He or she creates, instead, a visual antipathy, a recoil from the architectural remnants of a shared history: common floor levels, dimensions, window positions, and the like.

Such an effect is evident at 36-38 Jalan Haji Alias, for example. This is a pair of semis that we have christened the "Bi-Polar House." It is a clear study in contrasts. The manic side (opposite, at the left) appears overblown and overbuilt, with a full compliment of grandiose gestures and miniature luxuries: feature cladding, large-pane glazing, and cantilevered glass swimming pool. Its depressive twin, by contrast, is darkened with bronze windows, heavy curtains, and a defensive armature of burglar bars. One half projects an image that is hysterical, profligate, and highly social, while the other appears introverted, and vaguely pessimistic.

The form of the houses shows that they were created identical, palindromic, and mirrored across their party wall. The height of the houses is the same, and the roofs match exactly. The balcony floors are coplanar, and window openings on both levels are of similar size and proportion. These common origins dramatize the contrast found today. The manic house suggests a quality of excess—it has grown irrepressible, exuberant and slightly inappropriate. Like the manic individual, it seems to dilate and swell past its boundaries. All of its basic components are present in its morose double, albeit here in an engorged form. The corner turret is a perfect instance. Clearly this component

was once the same at either side. On the depressive house, this piece feels unambitious, an extension of its plastic materiality, the undifferentiated surfaces and soffits of the larger composition. The manic house re-presents this element so as to appear quasi-independent, a doodad. As elsewhere on the manic side, we find an over-elaboration of surface; the turret is clad with a medley of stones that is itself a "feature."

The manic house appears to propose itself to the passersby; its transparency, from the pool to the windows of the façade, borders on exhibitionism. It treats each of its elements as singular, fragmentary and demonstrative—as an ecstatic and dislocated experiential moment. These stand in unassimilated relationship to one another. By contrast, the depressive house expresses its massing as a sober whole. Where its neighbor is a jumble of events, the depressive house is a self-referential totality. This is made clear in the uncompromising plasticity of its material, which admits not even the articulation of joints. It is mute and non-

36-38 Jalan Haji Alias, Singapore

tectonic; slab edges run into soffits, into walls and eaves and parapets without delineation. Even the color of the windows conspires to minimize their contrast with the exterior plasterwork. At the same time, its accumulation of layers (glazing, grillwork, and curtains) downplays transparency.

It is amusing, moreover, to note that this bi-polarity extends into the landscape at the street. In front of an eye-catching feature wall, the manic house offers a colorful presentation of grass and variegated shrubs. The depressive garden is dun-colored and stunted. It seems appropriate, likewise, that the gray workmanlike convenience of a public wiring box would stand just this side of the party wall. In all senses its image is one of defeat; its neighbor, one of triumphalism.

The irony of the "warring" double is this: as each half strains for self-expression, it appears ever more bound by circumstance. The breakaway semi only emphasizes the originary bond with its conjoined twin, the albatross of its entanglements and attachments. In fact, the most effective dissembling done by the semi-detached house is in its original European form, where both sides cooperate in the illusion of a single large house. In this version, the party wall has no expression on the outside. Much like those London "apart-ments" that are lodged within ambiguous envelopes, these borrow the greatness of the larger structure while being deliberately evasive about their own extents. The illusion of wealth is sustained, paradoxically, through the hiding of the individual.

Some of the best English examples were clever enough to present the double-home not as a mirroring, but as a single, eccentrically disposed composition of bays and

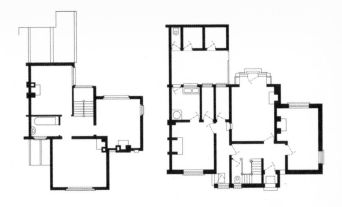

setbacks, turrets and secondary masses. Although each half is given an equal allotment of floor area, their organizations vary to reinforce the illusion of dissymmetry. The two sides diverge, but the effect is entirely opposite: the dissimilar halves mask the double behind a rangy architectural composition. This might be called a "schizoid" semi, in which one home is quietly, internally sheared into two discrete entities—and as such perhaps fits better in the category of the Trojan Horse (below).

The conjoined house is not a conventional beauty; certainly, it lacks the excessive beauty of other *unheimlich* doubles. But it is nonetheless grist for some interesting compositional possibilities. There may be a broken, buried or latent reflection. Mirroring is here interesting precisely when it becomes inexact. Elements remain recognizable in their shared origins—but they are subject to inversions, contradictions, inappropriate embellishments and skillful deceptions.

The potential interest of this condition is realized in projects such as the House House, designed by Johnston Marklee for a site in Inner Mongolia. As with Moneo's Kursaal, the building skillfully refuses resolution: this time, into either single or double. Its degree of integration

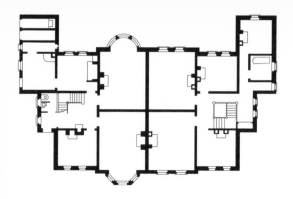

changes as one rotates around the exterior. An elegant cut appears to momentarily resolve the two halves into a single, stereotomic mass; elswhere, the composition seems to have quite obviously been designed as a symmetrical, conjoined pair. The House House stands alongside other engaged twins, such as Alejandro Aravena's Siamese Tower, which similarly destabilizes the traditional unity of the tower, creating a new paradigm for high-rise architecture. Rather than opting for a diagram, the architects of these works have understood the possibilities of the type, and have opted instead for a very productive instability.

The clone is a close relation of the double—the double of the double, as it were. These tropes occupy a common spectrum, one that locates problems of uniqueness and identity, of shared anatomies and genetic codes.

But the horror of cloning raises issues of mass repetition that, in both architecture and the broader culture, deserve special consideration. As Walter Benjamin and others note, reproduction—of people and objects, fake and real—is a pressing subject of late, and no less in modern architecture. For this reason, the clone remains a touchstone of the uncanny. It was for Freud, earlier,

Asymmetrical semi-detached pair, from Middleton, as above

who thought the reduplication of objects and events to be *unheimlich*. This included "unintended repetition," and "ghastly multiplication."[1] Freud shivered at the notion of endlessly re-encountering the same people and places, of stumbling, after Warhol or Nietzsche, through an "eternal recurrence of the same."[3]

Cloning suggests a mode of reproduction that is fundamentally in- or post-human, as does the undifferentiated character of its offspring. This discomfort has been subject to extensive treatment in 20th-century media, with renewed interest in the wake of genomic breakthroughs. Works such as Aldous Huxley's *Brave New World* conjectured that the clone could never be considered properly human, and would be fodder for exploitation—for example, to labor for a leisure class. Others imagine the commodification of the cloned body itself, as a means for the harvesting of organs. This was visualized in the 1979 cult film *Parts: The Clonus Horror*, in *The Island* (2005), and more famously in Kazuo Ishiguro's *Never Let Me Go*. In a sense, the clone is a kind of "bare life," a body without a soul—not a human, but pieces thereof. Artificial beings, like the replicants in *Blade Runner*, are external to the reproductive, and hence the social, order.

The clone has been a particular preoccupation of that ur-modern product, the cinema. This is quite natural, perhaps, as film allows a convincing illusion of cloning through multiple exposures, a device that links Georges Méliès to the Michael Keaton comedy *Multiplicity*. But replication is also inherent in the medium itself: as recurrences of frames that are unified within the memory of the eye, viewed on multiple occasions, and distributed across geographical space.

Just as much, perhaps, cloning is inherent in the productive matrix of modern architecture. Buildings, and their components, have come to be replicated on a mass scale. Architects have made a virtue of necessity, often embracing repetition with a religious fervor. The architecture of mass production is said to have "arrived" in Peter Behrens' A.E.G. turbine factory of 1909, famously a temple of extrusion in which the building, and the process it embodied, were united in their expression. Behrens' shed comprised identical bays, simply placed side by side, to the length required by the assembly lines within.

The placement of duplicate segments in horizontal, vertical, or gridded arrays has remained, for years, the basic DNA of construction. Images of Hilberseimer façades have perhaps been over-used in representing this vocabulary. Regardless, such buildings exist—not least, in "public" housing everywhere: the lugubrious slab of the Parisian *banlieu*, the London council estate, the Singaporean "HDB," or the high-rise priapolis of São Paulo (*saudade do futuro,* with balconies). Some instances have taken this to almost sardonic lengths, as in the anthills of Hong Kong, or Saenz de Oiza's kilometer-long "El Ruedo" complex along Madrid's M-30 (1986).

The architect's courtship of mass manufacture reached an apex in the modularity movements, in "prefab" and Metabolism. Here, the "capsule"—be it a room, an apartment, or a fully constructed dwelling—is delivered from factory to site, and agglomerates as a conjoined clone. Moishe Safdie's Habitat (1967) arrayed its units in a kind of techno-primitive pile; likewise, the configurations of Kisho Kurokawa's BC25 Capsule gave it life as part of high-rises, as vacation cottages and nomadic urban caravans. In each, the conglomerate is imagined as a hive of like elements, an economy of scale.

In fact, repetition is not unique to "mature" Modernism. It is seen in London's Georgian streets, speculative developments built on land seized from the church in Henry VIII's reformation.[4] Row-housing was also a product of 18th-century Paris and Victorian England, as well as Edwardian New York and 1920s Shanghai.

With the "subdivisions" of the post-war American suburb came other landscapes of minimally different houses. Franchise-communities such as Levittown introduced the famous "little boxes" arrayed along a circuitry of curves and cul-de-sacs. Here, dwellings truly became industrial commodities, alongside their components. And awkward

(above) Aerial photo of Levittown, New Jersey (left) Walter Gropius & Otto Haesler, Dammerstock Siedlung Karsruhe

problems arose. The suburb embodied uniformity, but not unity. There existed no connective tissue to make them whole: no reciprocity between buildings, no hierarchy of scale or language, and no larger urban figure apart from the neutral ladder of roads.[5] These "nuclear" family houses remain anomic, separated by the indeterminate surface of the lawn.

The other great example of cloned housing, the "terrace," faces a similar problem. This type is now global. It remains a compact option for the development of low-rise urban parcels, and strange new versions continue to arise. The streetscapes of Chicago's Old Town and Lincoln Park, for example, have been unhappily transformed by the "prairie po-mo" terrace, which exhibits a forced play of surface treatments and eccentric pediments.[6] Singapore has also been a site of experiment in the modernization of rowhouses, where the single row is bent into branching or bronchial arrangements, as in the Shanghai *nongtang*.

These conjoined clones should be distinguished from the block of flats, which is in many ways a less agonized problem. While also a repetitive composition, the modern apartment building frequently presents itself as a singular, though complex, object. It represents a sublation of the "unit" within a collective; in essence, *uniformity*

Walter Gropius, "Honeycomb" Building System

is its aesthetic problem. The block of flats resembles the European semi or the skillfully deceptive London accommodation. In these, the dwelling has been dissolved into a larger object.

By contrast, the terrace must attempt to resolve the hairy predicament of the proto-house: a gathering of pieces, defined by adjacencies. The rowhouse (like the semi) struggles in the limen between one and many. It is often too narrow to be expressed as a house in its own right. Rather, as its frontage is compressed, it appears as a component of one.[8] This does not stop the effort to make it appear as a "proper" domicile, and the results remain ham-strung between the expression of the house and of something new. This is the case in Boston's South End, for example, where the home is a sort of contraction. The bay window stands abreast of others, its neighbors, as houses might be arrayed along a street.

As urbanism, the terrace attempts to collect a busyness of house-fragments into a whole. Unification has been attempted, and sometimes achieved, via a range of techniques: a defining material or color, an unusual roof form, a repeated element or iconographic theme. Such is the case at FAT's Lindsay Road housing in Sheffield, UK, where outsized ornament incorporates a collection of small

FAT, Lindsay Road Housing, Sheffield

homes. Through a tactical and witty deployment, these elements turn repetition into meaningful urbanism, making distinctions at corners and edges, interiors and perimeters. Large-order massing gestures can likewise create coherence, as in the curves of Herzog and de Meuron's Pilotengasse housing in Vienna. These work hard to overcome an awkwardness inherent to the type—a pull between family and collectivity, "indivisibility [and] individuality."[10] The worst cases present urbanism as proximity without society, Emile Durkheim's notion of *anomie* in built form.[11]

We can see this clearly at Corona Court in Singapore, from 1984. It is poignant that this terrace, an object defined by the act of living together, should be expressed as a symphony of boundaries. Party walls stand proud of the façade, and frontages are staggered such that they do not align. This makes them appear to resist incorporation within a unified block. Paradoxically, these are intended to work as a motif, a repetition that makes the complex read as a whole. They both join and separate.

Terraces, despite such efforts to unify them, appear most peculiar at their ends, where repetition must end in a pleasing urban resolution. This is not easy to do, and requires rather muscular gestures. There remains something eerily uncontained about these buildings. They embody a dangerous fertility: like "triffids," or some meristematic material that spreads *ad infinitum*. The size of a row appears conditional: it could be more, or less. Perhaps for this reason, terraces are often ambiguously terminated with the blank expression of a party wall.

The interesting ambiguities of the clone may yet be redeemed, however. They are exploited in the works of Peter Eisenman, for example, which often employ repeated units as a compositional device and a basis for experiment. This allows the progressive reading of formal operations applied to similar objects. Evolving distortions are legible in a series of bars or boxes, arrayed or conjoined in rows or grids. Eisenman's clones are imperfect—in fact, they are more like a hereditary sequence, subject to identity and also to change. This can be seen in his Carnegie Mellon Research Institute (1988), where a module is created via a "genetic" process of rotation and superimposition. The masses appear similar, but are only superficially so: in fact, they are differentially intersected by a framework of structural members.[13] A more overt sequence can be seen in block studies for the Rebstockpark Masterplan in Frankfurt (1990), where repeated masses are subject to subtle deformation across oblique lines of transformation.[14] This technique is less convincing in the Columbus Convention Center (1993), in which the cloned elements, linear bands that break the mass into stripes, simply wiggle. Their movement creates minor variations, but is not deeply transformative. In each case, however, Eisenman's distortions balance the exception against the norm, in such a way that the former enables the reading of the latter.

Victor Bourgeois, Cité Moderne, Brussels

1

This recalls, again, our notion of the horrible multiple as both one and many, freak and exemplar, individual and type. As "monstrous singularity" and "case," as well as the intimation of an emergent new order. Twins and clones challenge notions of conformity by copying *too immediately, too aggressively, and too well*; their replication and consanguinity becomes, itself, a potentially destabilizing kind of deviance.

2

1. Typical rowhouse plans, after Middleton 2. Eisenman
Architects, Carnegie Mellon Research Institute, Pittsburgh
3. Aldine Terrace, Chicago 4. Corona Court, Singapore

Exquisite Corpse

*"Be glad thou art not...an heteroclite in nature,
with some member defective or redundant... Be glad
that thy clay-cottage hath all the necessary rooms
thereto belonging, though the outside be not so fairly
plastered as some others."*
Thomas Fuller, "On Deformity."[1]

*"Who knows...how many suffering, crippled,
fragmentary forms of life there are, such as the
artificially created life of chests and tables quickly
nailed together, crucified timbers, silent martyrs to
human inventiveness. The terrible transplantation
of incompatible and hostile races of wood, their
merging into one misbegotten personality..."*
Bruno Schulz[2]

The exquisite corpse is a type of horror through
which another problem of singularity and collectivity—
the death of the unified building—is expressed.

Its name refers to a parlor game, associated with
André Breton and the Parisian Surrealists. A folded sheet
of paper was passed between participants, each of whom
contributed a drawing, word or phrase without knowledge
of what came before. When opened, there were surprising
combinations, fragmented figures that gleefully subverted
norms of painterly coherence. This technique raised the
liberating prospect that a single work might combine
multiple authors, contents, and modes of representation. Its
results surpassed even the fragmentary aspirations of the
Cubists, who worked to capture their subjects at multiple,

1. André Breton, Yves Tanguy, Jacqueline Lamba, *Exquisite Corpse*, c. 1938   2. Brett Murray, *Africa*, Cape Town, South Africa, 1998
3. Collectible figurines of Hieronymous Bosch's *The Last Judgment*

(above) Hans Poelzig, Lowenburg Town Hall
(below) Andreas Gursky, *Copan*, 2002

overlapping spatio-temporal positions. These double-exposures were complex and anxious; for the surrealists the modern object became downright schismatic.

The rise of this sort of disjunctive aesthetics—as well as the shock and horror associated with it—became urgent at a certain point in the experience of modernity. The term *collage* itself, from *coller* or "glue," is attributed to a circle that included Picasso and Braque. Fore-tremors were felt in the juxtaposed patterns of dandyism, or the eclecticism of the Victorian interior. But the latter lacked the strident disjuncture of the collage, still framed within the ornamental equilibrium of the Neoclassical.

When applied to actual bodies, the compositional logic of the exquisite corpse has produced striking images of deviant anatomy. The archetypal "heteroclite" might be Frankenstein, jerry-rigged from pilfered limbs and organs. Stitches are the stigmata of his condition, lines of abrupt and unholy dis-articulation. The "tatterdemalion" is not a full being but a sum of parts: a complete body, but an incomplete self. He lacks a soul, as his animating spirit is electricity. This image was timely. Mary Shelley wrote for an age in which the electrical experiments of Erasmus Darwin—and the theories of "animal magnetism" first claimed by Franz Anton Mesmer[3]—were reordering notions of the body and its operating energies. Galvanism suggested the possibility of reanimation, a subject fictionalized by H.P. Lovecraft and lampooned by Edgar Allan Poe.

Shelley's golem emerged as a prescient nightmare of modern medical science, a century before fragmented paintings became an icon of modern shock. Numerous living inventors—among them René Descartes, Jacques de

Vaucanson and Thomas Edison—were described as a "new Prometheus" for assembling automata out of cloth, feathers, fur, and mechanical parts.[4] Public concern consumed these objects. The French predictably focused upon Vaucanson's replication of the duck's digestion. If peristalsis could be produced, would not cogitation follow?

By later (and earlier) standards, the image of Frankenstein looks coherent. His form is still human, his pieces largely proportionate. In most films, his body does not look mismatched so much as pale and cadaverous, scarred and clunky. Others have done much worse in pushing the limits of the singular anatomy. The bizarre iterations of John Carpenter's *The Thing* (1982), for example, limns the limits of biomorphic possibility. In its gestational phases, it is so garbled as to be non-functioning. During a canine phase, the alien is a limping sack, a heavily veined scrotum with vestigial limbs and arachnid legs. Hand-like appendages and a dog's face grow out of its top. These components clearly hail from creatures of differing kingdoms—hairy, human, or invertebrate.

Hieronymous Bosch and François Rabelais pioneered such nightmares in the medium of carnival grotesque, imagining a polymorphy of obscene and bestial combinations. These built upon folk tradition, the wild excesses described by M.M. Bakhtin. Sanctioned transgressions included the interpolation of human and animal anatomies, honorifics lent to fauna, and double-images of religious personages and their wild avatars.

Here, the body is not singular, but a collective. It is a disgusting little society, one in which the members are awkwardly or inimically related. In the most sanguine reading, this "social body" suggests an uneasy democracy.

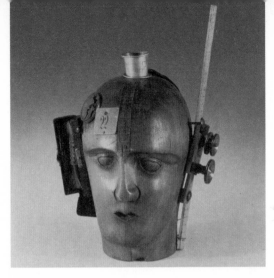

It recalls Chantal Mouffe's "agonistic" *demos,* a kind of unstable compact in which the constituents are unified only through a re-staging of their difference. It likewise echoes the rabble of Aristotle's *Politics.* All the limbs wish to move in different directions. Here also, in dismal form, is Bruno Latour's famous "parliament of nature."

A more recent version explores the violence of the human-machine interface. This is the staple of Japanese body horror, of films such as *Machine Girl* (2008) and Shinya Tsukamoto's cult *Tetsuo the Iron Man* (1989). In these, severed limbs are replaced with working machinery and weapons, and bodily cavities are filled with gears, pumps and pistons. Quentin Tarantino covered this genre in "Death Proof," a segment of the *Grindhouse* film (2007). Here, a machine gun stands in the place of a severed leg. As in the Asian precedents, the inserted element is not prosthetic: it does not attempt to replace a missing anatomical member so much as to impose an awkward and dangerous substitute. Here, juxtaposition of flesh and metal creates a sort of weaponized pornography. This imagery

Raoul Haussmann, "Der Geist Unserer Zeit," c.1920

hearkens back directly to the original use of mechanical pieces in collages by the Dada and Surrealist groups, as icons of post-human creep. The most familiar is perhaps Raoul Hausmann's "Mechanischer Kopf" (c.1920), a freakish parody of the Hellenic (and Humanist) bust.

These works are useful when one examines architectural experiments of late, and particularly those that rely upon fragmentation. It is not an overstatement to suggest that the failure of the modern monad is one of the discipline's major preoccupations since the 1970s. Some of the most celebrated contemporary projects appear driven by the reintroduction of diversity into the box.

The freedom to deny the coherence of the building opens interesting avenues for exploration. This is an obvious source of joy in the work of Robert Venturi and Denise Scott Brown, where contradiction offered an opportunity to challenge the artificiality of conventions. In the Lieb House (1969), for example, the aggressive disjunction of bottom and top, and the rough and partial quotation of windows and openings, suggests not a complete "design" but a gathering of recycled components. The Allen Memorial Art Museum at Oberlin College (1976) likewise plays with disjuncture, but does so in the abrupt transition of facades around corners.

A similar technique is employed at James Stirling and Michael Wilford's Clore Wing at the Tate Gallery (1980-87). The small courtyard created by the architects somehow supports a riot of façades, frames, and variegated windows around its perimeter. While the main entrance quotes the stone pediments of the original Tate, a non-structural grid is dominant elsewhere. Like the striation of the Arthur M. Sackler Museum (1979-84), this provides a

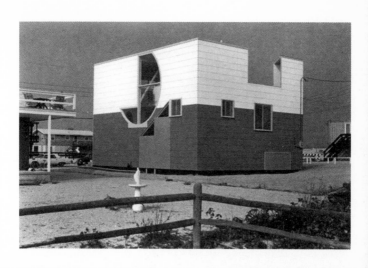

(above) Venturi Scott Brown, Lieb House   (below) James Stirling
and Michael WIlford, Clore Wing, Tate Gallery, London, sketch

loose system against which openings are allowed to play. The grid extends the materiality of the stone, albeit in a playful way.

The high-analytical technique of VSB and Stirling takes on a somewhat more poetic, although no less cerebral, iteration in the work of Aldo Rossi. The exquisite corpse is here a creature of mental life, a piebald social history of architecture. Memories and quotations, embodied in typologies and iconography, become en-tangled in a Freudian mechanism of condensation. As in "dream-work," a compositing and a reduction occur. Like a vision from Bruno Schulz's tales, the Rossian object appears to congeal wishful images, nostalgic ephemera, and cultural reverberations. Aggregation is the principal compositional technique, here—and Rossi's oneirics are also a kind of magical urbanization. We begin to lose sight of what is building and what is city. In a forecasting of Koolhaas, the line becomes obscured. This is clear, for example, in the Terranova Commercial Centre (1996-7); a pavilion at the Fiera di Verona (1996); Schützenstrasse Berlin (1992-8); and Whitehall Ferry Terminal, New York (1992). Sadly, a similar approach results in a series of crudely referential objects in the hands of others: Jeremy Dixon's St. Mark's Road Housing (1975), Ricardo Bofill's Palace of Abraxas (1978-80), or Michael Graves' extension to the Whitney Museum in New York (1987).

Frank Gehry likewise explores the potentials of the exquisite corpse; but in doing so provides a stark contrast to the wistful Rossian spirit. His Norton Residence in Venice Beach (1982-84) uses nautical fragments, as well as the bric-a-brac of the Californian home, to dramatize the chaos of Los Angeles' anti-context. In the manner of the surrounding plots, each of Norton's pieces are treated as distinct and independent, culminating in the roadside study that echoes lifeguard stations on the beach. Gehry deploys his pieces with a radical casualness, and varying degrees of misappropriation and overstatement. Potentially kitsch elements—such as blue pool tiles, or the mock-monumental *torii*—are reframed in an original way. Into this "junkyard" quilt, the architect places a wide array of quotations from American building: wood siding, shingles, standing-seam roofing, etc.

Despite the retreat of such signification—in Gehry's practice, as well as in the discipline at large—the exquisite corpse nonetheless reached a second peak in the Dutch architecture of the 1990s. Here, the collage technique came to be thoroughly applied in plan and section. Rem Koolhaas and his peers have tended to subdivide the total building: its diverse contents—programs, materials, and structures—are placed in novel distributions and combinations. These create a rich interior life. As in the best works of Venturi and Scott Brown or Stirling and Wilford, the surprising potentials of the exquisite corpse are exhaustively explored.

In many projects, fragmentation is ordered by means of a graphical device, a kind of "built diagram." This was the case with a landscape of stripes in the Parc de la Villette competition (1982), and in an array of projects in the subsequent decade that employed similar programmatic collages. However, this device was used with such skill that a diverse repertoire flourished. Breton's magical anti-system allowed a freedom to pursue the local: once a compositional method was developed, the building could exult in the production of event, accident, singularity, and

(above) Frank Gehry, Lewis Residence, Lyndhurst, Ohio
(below) Frank Gehry, Norton House, Venice, California

character. The building is effectively urbanized. Such as strategy is evident, for example, in the McCormick Tribune Campus Center at IIT (2003), which resembles certain of Mies' own abstract collages of volumes and their contents.[7]

The imposition of variety is even more strident in the work of MVRDV. The buildings of Winy Maas follow a similar tactical trajectory those of Koolhaas. Some of these—such as the headquarters for VPRO in Hilversum, in the Netherlands (1998)—do not utilize fragmentation so much as they pursue the variability of a common element, such as the warped floor. In other examples, the exquisite corpse comes dramatically to the fore. Such was Maas's Netherlands Pavilion for the 2000 Hanover Expo. A collection of landscapes were stacked vertically, each level a marked disjuncture from that above or below. A key gesture was the lack of a unifying element in the composition. Rather, the casual stacking functions , itself, as a kind of plastic collage.

The Netherlands Pavilion, perhaps more than any other building, approaches a purified analogue of the exquisite corpse. Stacking is pursued quite brutally, and each level is independent. This differs from Koolhaas' Kunsthal, in which synthetic compositional gestures remain. In the latter, a structural grid provides a kind of unifying veil, a light or "gay" systematization.[8] The grid is subject to the specific gravity of elements, and columns drift and transform. By contrast, the Pavilion opens into a vortex, a final abandonment of the last gestures of totality. It embodies pure "negative freedom," the right of the architect to be constrained by nothing apart from the technical or the budgetary.

1. Arby's breakfast sandwich 2.MVRDV, Netherlands Pavilion, Hannover Expo 2000 3. Kris Kuksi, *Church Tank Type 8*, 2007

"Long live the new flesh!"
James Woods, *Videodrome*

The exquisite corpse is characterized by an unmediated adjacency: its varied parts are casually placed side-by-side. Their meeting, at lines of transformation, is nigh-magical. The compositional language of collage is, itself, the organizing factor. It provides a visible coherence, while appearing to grant its constituent pieces total freedom to be what they will.

In some cases, however, the hybrid composition betrays an attempt at synthesis. Some common substance embraces the riot of parts. This may be a skin; a material such as brick or concrete; a contiguity or logic of shape or geometry; an iconographic enclosure, or the invocation of a genetic process. It may also occur through an attempt to temper the alienation of the fragments, by creating an echo of resemblance among them. The haircut known as the "mullet" is a good example. This object clearly combines two incompatible aesthetics: "business in the front" and "party in the back." However, the mullet is precisely not an exquisite corpse. Hair itself provides a common medium— short and long are part of the same surface.

Ungrammatical anatomies are very old. Authors such as Dante, Rabelais, and Nikolai Gogol[1] have left lasting images. The gruesome possibilities have been most graphically exploited, perhaps, in the film genre of "body horror," wherein the normal physique undergoes rapid and shocking transformations. David Cronenberg's *The Fly* (1986), for example, lingers graphically over the unstable genetic meld of scientist Seth Brundle (Jeff Goldblum) and an insect. Films such as *Shivers* (1975), *The Brood* (1979) and

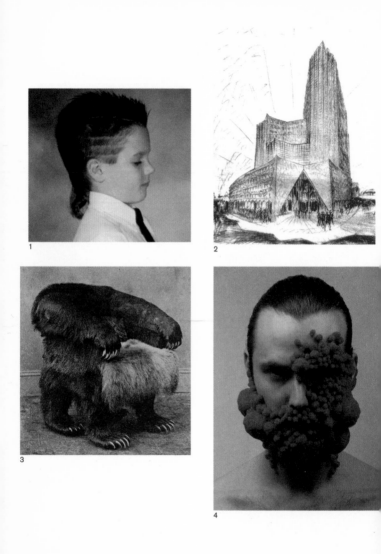

1. Mullet   2. Hans Scharoun, Friedrichstrasse Skyscraper, 1921   3. Grizzly bear chair for Andrew Johnson, 1865   4. Lucy McRae, *Grow on You*, 2010

Henrique Olivera, *Tapumes - Casa dos Leões*, 2009

The Human Centipede (2010) explored a similar eclipse of the singular, bounded human.

This has been more poetically (but no less acutely) imagined in certain works by contemporary artists, in which the body or the building become the site of interplay for two different anatomical modes: a "norm" and an aberration. This is the case in the work of Lucy McRae and Bart Hess, for example, where the face and torso become colonized by wool, wood, and plantings in a virus-like emergence. It is perhaps most arresting in the installations of Henrique Oliveira, where the familiar appearance of architectural environments—the gallery, and also the "traditional" urban fragment—are counterposed with large-scale biomorphic elements. Works such as *Tapumes - Casa dos Leões* (2009) are, since those of Paul Thek, the most sublime in their juxtaposition of different media and bodily logics.

Such assemblies are unnerving, in part, because they contravene norms of body-making. Due to the rigors of the evolutionary process, anatomy usually appears to us as having a certain formal coherence, or logic. In terms of aesthetics, we follow Darwin in his belief that *natura non facit saltum*: the genetic doesn't make awkward leaps or jarring transitions.

We find this form of horror in architectures from transitional moments, at thresholds in the evolution of design languages. Or, during phases in which social and geopolitical transformation, such as colonial expansion, created a fashion for the acquisitive. In Georgian Britain and Renaissance Italy, for example, the inclusion of foreign elements took place in the creation of follies, urban set-pieces, and other exceptional architectures. The stylistic imperium of New York at the turn of the last century absorbed a hodgepodge of ornamental styles—Moorish, Sumerian, Gothic, and many others—and stuffed them into the composition of the skyscraper and retail block.

Early modern examples of this are striking. Michael de Klerk's brilliant housing block and post office for the Eigen Haard Association in Amsterdam (1917-21), exploits to full advantage the potentials of heterodox anatomy. The intersection of Dutch conventions with a wildly imaginative early modern style allows for a sort of satisfying mannerism rarely seen since. Here, the jumbled accretions of the medieval block intersect with a kind of *heimlich* organicism. An overall architectural expression establishes links with a vernacular European language of construction: brickwork, tile roofs, and a perimeter block of normative fenestration. However, this is merely a loose framework, and into this permissive structure de Klerk inserts a cadenza of unusual elements. Bulging bay projections; nautical ligatures that recall keels, prows and hulls, and rhetorical roofs that appear to hail from different eras. De Klerk's brick surface undergoes multiple transformations in order to enclose these divergent geometries—distributions alternate in a *tour de force* of articulation. The surface is lively and serpentine, its bonds stretching to accommodate bulbous turrets and cylindrical chimney stacks. The tension between character elements and the larger composition—as well as between housing, post office and public areas—is the source of much poetic richness.

The Chilehaus (1920-24) by Fritz Höger is likewise a transitional object, one that plays a vestigial classicism against radical abstraction. Here we find a casual

1 and 2., Housing block and post office for the Eigen Haard Association, Amsterdam 3. Fritz Höger, Chilehaus, Hamburg

use of traditional elements, such as cornices and sash windows, but these are deployed within a curvilinear Brick Expressionism. The airfoil massing appears to accelerate toward an acute corner. Within it are situated, surprisingly, the stolid windows of the Germanic perimeter block, arrayed in an unrelenting grid. The walls flanking the razor-sharp prow are only one bay wide, and the topmost window has a semi-circular top—seen in isolation, this fragment could be Georgian, or perhaps borrowed from a Shanghainese Art Deco compound such as Huai Hai Fang (c. 1920). These strategies lend the total form a reading that appears to contradict the facades—the static and abstract character of the latter sits strangely against what is, elsewhere, a celebration of speed.[2]

More recently, Frank Gehry has provided many of the most notable examples of a return to synthesis, as opposed to the purer language of fragmentation in his work of the 1970s and early 1980s. Where projects such as the Gehry House (1978), Norton House (1984), Loyola Law School (1984) and Winton Guest House (1987) play up their contrasts of form and material, the Schnabel House (1989), Weisman Museum (1993), and Vitra Design Museum (1989) immerse the fragmented shapes in a common medium.

In some cases, the impression of the ungrammatical body can approach that of the conjoined twin. This is most clear when it includes only two elements. The "warring" semi-detached house, for example, might appear as a form of ungrammatical body.[3] In fact, the conjoined twin presents the unnatural bonding of two individuals who are substantially the same. The emphasis of the ungrammatical body remains the *singular* being, oddly composed.

Ungrammar as doubling appears, for example, in the Santuario De Nuestra Señora De Las Lajas in Ipiales, Colombia (1916-1949). Here, a basilica and bridge were built together, spanning a canyon of the Guáitara River. However, an examination of the building reveals that it is not to be simply understood as a church sitting on a viaduct—however odd this would be. The overpass extends from a level roughly halfway up the height of the structure; rooms continue below, as does Romanesque fenestration that has clearly been designed to echo what stands above. This would suggest a single object, a meld of infrastructure and building. However, the instability of this proposition makes the result more suggestive. Note, for example, that the bridge has not simply been "assumed" into the composition. It does not merely jut out, like a car porch or canopy. Rather, it is a strong organizational datum, and the material treatment of the Santuario—as well as the intensity of its ornamentation—transforms across this line. Above, the materiality is delicate and embellished. Below, it is rugged and rustic. There is a fascinating visual contradiction at work; one is unsure whether to interpret the totality as two discrete horizontal strata, or as a very vertical building with a horizontal addendum. Neither reading is, in fact, supportable. The former is invalidated by the continuation of the church architecture (albeit in ruder form) below the bridge. The latter seems implausible due to the emphatic doubling of architectural vocabularies. This is to say, Nuestra Senora de Las Lajas cannot be interpreted according to the two most obvious grammatical conventions that would relate its parts to its totality. Rather, it is one body, "incorrectly" assembled.

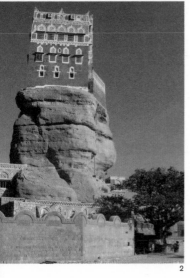

1. Nuestra Senora De Las Lajas, Ipiales, Colombia 2. Dar Al Hajar, Yemen
3. Furness & Evans, First National Bank of the Republic, Philadelphia

Partially and Mostly Dead

The literature of fear is replete with characters that are multiple. And also with those that are, to various degrees, dead. Take the zombie, whose body continues to labor under a horrid automatism after the soul and intellect have been evicted. Or the vampire, who—as the vile inversion of Christ—has conquered death by feeding on the vitality of the living.[1] Less fantastically, a similar unease is focused upon partially necrotic individuals: amputees, paraplegics and quadriplegics, sufferers of paralysis, lepers, and even "vegetative" persons. The victim of terminal illness has likewise been stigmatized for bringing death into life, for having "one foot in the grave." As Georges Canguilhem pointed out, it is not long since clinical definitions of pathology were focused upon a quantification of "morbidity" among the living.

By analogy, the moribund cityscape produces some striking imagery, steeped in the romance of ruin. For example, ongoing warfare between FARC guerillas and the national military in Colombia has given rise to a number of temporary and permanent ghost towns. Villages such as La Union Peneya were forcibly decamped, their houses left with food on the table and radios playing.[2] A few residents dared to remain, alone. The 1974 de-occupation of Varosha, in contested territory between Greek and Turkish Cyprus, was similarly abrupt. This formerly chic

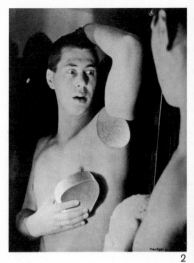

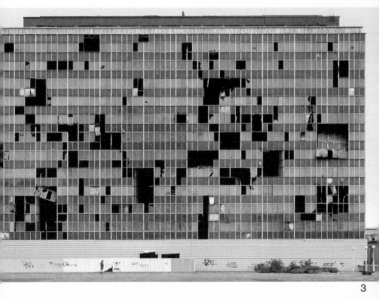

1 "Nancy Linton," victim of patent medicine, c. 1833   2. Herbert Bayer, *Humanly Impossible*, 1932   3. Filip Dujardin, from the series *Fictions*, 2010

1

2

1. Abandoned floor, Bonn   2. Takashi Kuribayashi, "For Aquarium: I Feel Like I Am In A Fishbowl!", 2006   3. Ruyungyung Hotel, Pyongyang   4. Mountain Farms Mall, Hadley, MA   5. Partially destroyed buildings, Shanghai, 2004

3

4

5

vacation spot—a favorite of Brigitte Bardot—moldered as an improvised demilitarized zone, its streets growing with beach grass. The image recalls Andrei Tarkovsky's *Stalker* (1979), in which nature begins to reclaim a Soviet town in the wake of an unnamed incident. A similar atmosphere hovers at Gunkanjima ("Battleship Island"), a coal-mining town located 15 kilometers off the coast of the Nagasaki Peninsula, in the East China Sea. The Japanese government completed its depopulation in 1974, and the resulting decay of high-density concrete architecture has given the outpost new life as a popular attraction for tourists.

The urban world is full of such necrotic topologies. Jeremiads have focused on the decline of Milwaukee, Baltimore, and Cleveland. But also downtown Johannesburg, "spectral" Kinshasa, Ciudad Juárez and Sheffield, among many others. Here, the archetype of the mostly dead building is the abandoned dwelling or squat. Urban nightmares of "the ghetto" and "the projects" commonly fix upon wasted lots and apartments, either destroyed or home to that proto-zombie, the junkie or crackhead. Likewise, in post-Katrina New Orleans, imagery has conflated water-damaged houses and the drowned. The fear is of death ascendant, seizing pockets of the urban lifeworld, just next door. Detroit is often cited as the singularly terminal figure, a discursive opposite to the "vibrant" city fabric. Indeed, one finds here extraordinary instances of dereliction and waste. These include not only houses, but also the grandest examples of civic building: Michigan Central Station, United Artists' Theatre and Old First Unitarian Church. These are perhaps rivaled only by Pyongyang's Ryungyung Hotel, a pyramidal high-rise that loomed, empty, above the skyline as from 1992 to 2008.

Less rarefied examples exist, also. In America, one of the more visible metrics of devaluation is the so-called "dead mall." The suburban and "rurban" landscape contains many examples. The visitor can read their degree of morbidity through vacant units, as well as the presence of sub-prime tenants. Notable specimens include the Brickyard Mall in Chicago; Assembly Square Mall in Somerville, Massachusetts; and the famous Sherman Oaks Galleria in Los Angeles, which served as the set for *Fast Times at Ridgemont High* (1982). The death of the mall is commonly marked by a slow decline, in which surviving units abut empty ones. Typically, owners and management attempt to fend off total closure, but devaluation is endemic to the high turnover of the commercial real estate cycle. Continual demand for one-stop shopping appears to result in ever larger consolidations and newly built centers. Regardless, abandonment occurs alongside an occasional dramatic renaissance.[3] There is sometimes a form of "morbid exchange," also: a transfer of value among competing facilities built near one another. This was the case of Mountain Farms mall in Hadley, MA, which was flatlining throughout the 1990s as a result of competition from the adjacent Hampshire Mall. An injection of higher-end chains—such as Barnes and Noble—has reversed this balance, with Mountain Farms returning the malignancy to its competitor.

Abandoned structures are often assumed to be haunted, and not merely by the apparition of poverty. In much of Asia, for example, accounts of spectral visitations thrive, and focus in particular upon deflated and devalued architecture. Such a stigma is logical with respect to "dead" space. Why otherwise would usable human inhabitations be left idle? Are these not the trysting-place of death and life? As with the partially necrotic, haunted houses are not merely—or even thoroughly—dead. Certainly they are vacant with respect to humans; but they are lively with memories, and homeless or unsettled spirits. They present the mixture of life and un-life in the same object. As Nabokov wrote, in *Terror*,

> "I looked at houses and they had lost their usual meaning...leaving nothing but an absurd shell... I understood the horror of a human face. Anatomy, sexual distinctions, the notion of "legs," "arms," "clothes,"—all that was abolished, and there remained in front of a mere *something*—not even a creature, for that too is a human concept, but merely *something* moving past."[4]

Buildings that appear spectral need not even be abandoned or destroyed. To be unoccupied is enough. Such is the case, for example, with the Singapore Telecom exchange at Hill Street, which combines the haunted house with the technical object. This looming metal tower is what is known as a "cable hotel," effectively a vertical convolution of telephone wiring, which sits improbably on a low podium of Islamic style. Its status as architecture is particularly ambiguous—not being a building for humans, it is subject to relatively few rules or conventions. It is a node at which zones of the city's telecommunications infrastructures come together. It is a mostly non-inhabited structure, divided into rooms that are filled with lines, switches and interfaces. The exchange seems not a building as much as a haunted technology. Disembodied voices pass here in conversation; signals speak to each other. Almost no one enters. Its location is arbitrary, its centralization (and central location) bizarre. Its dark rooms are full of chatter, silent and yet reverberant with speech. It is at once full and empty, a center of reference, gesturing toward life elsewhere.

Such objects—terminal malls, haunted houses and infrastructures, and devalued neighborhoods—are mostly dead. Perhaps equally horrid is the *partially* dead building. The latter should be distinguished from "not dead *yet*," a notion that will be familiar from the absurdisms of Camus and Monty Python. Instead, this is the problem of the quasi-deceased body, the missing limb or corporeal cavity. The abandoned house is like a corpse, within which yet flicker animations of the spirit. The *partially* dead building is occupied and vacated at the same time. It is like a damaged tree, which will stanch the flow of nutrients to a compromised limb, hastening its decomposition. Broken appendages are capped with a protective seal, leading to a proliferation of stumps and hollows: a kind of creepy anatomy in which life and death coexist in the same body. An analogous architecture, one partially decayed, is in certain ways more discomfiting than a total ruin. Such a building appears locally penetrated by death; it has "imbibed of the shadows of fallen columns," but has not succumbed.[5]

This condition often results, perhaps un-surprisingly, from the cold-blooded rationality of the economic. We see this, for example, in the contemporary practice of "decanting." In the United States and Asia, buildings that are undergoing renovation may decant part of their gross floor area (GFA)—that quantum upon which development charges are levied—by removing areas of floor plate. This has the effect of making pockets of space effectively uninhabitable. As developers pay municipal authorities on a per-area basis, the most effective way to "massage" the GFA is to amputate. This practice results in a series of ghostly voids, pockets of uncanny space that are abandoned. Strangely, the presence of inaccessible and hidden compartments is a mainstay of contemporary facilities planning, as it was of the literature of the fantastic: Lovecraft, E.T.A. Hoffmann, Poe, and Rudyard Kipling have all engaged the subject.

"Decanting" is a strategy of hotel renovations, in particular, where the flootage given to guest rooms is weighed against other profitable programs, such as restaurants and retail. Less profitable distributions are quickly and brutally rectified: the floor of a guest-room is cut away, and replaced with a non-structural material. As such, a sort of "ghost room" is inserted, partitioned by ceiling board. This combines a number of terrors: the sealed void; the floor that cannot support a person; the forbidden room. This occurs against the backdrop of the already horrifying hotel, a facility that mixes categories of personal and public, and implies all manner of seedy exchanges and violences. Its mechanical and bureaucratic character—its stacks of numbered cells—leads to a phantasmagoria of forgotten transgressions. This was clearly the case in Stanley Kubrick's *The Shining* (1980). But within the hotel trade itself, in Asia in particular, are stories in which haunted rooms are sealed off by management.[6]

Distaste for the idea of decanting reflects, perhaps, the ruthlessness of its logic. The term itself describes an emptying of the spirit in the name of fluidity. We are shocked to imagine that part of a "body," an inhabited object, might simply be voided and relegated to non-life. This echoes the Gothic horror of the only-partially-inhabited space, sealed attics or basements, and storage rooms. It recalls the nightmare sequence from Terry Gilliam's Brazil (1985), in which the maternal body opens to reveal a sort of smooth hollow containing fruit-like objects—in a manner reminiscent of Giles Deleuze's "body without organs."[7] This is disgusting. As Aristotle famously noted, nature abhors a vacuum.

The decanted space represents a sort of waste that is counter-intuitive to any logic outside the rentier. It seems unimaginable that usable rooms would be left in this way. However, the phenomenon is actually quite common. As elsewhere, German cities have seen a dramatic increase in such practices. In Bonn, for example, the second and third floor rooms of high-street buildings are commonly abandoned. The rental rates of different floors are so disproportionate that entire upper levels are valued less than the footprint of the stair at the ground. The stairs are thus often removed, and the spaces above abandoned. This is likewise the case in other major German cities. Even more poignant is a phenomenon documented by photographer Greg Girard in Shanghai, where spaces *and* their inhabitants are sometimes jettisoned. This is the condition of certain disabled elderly, who are placed in attic voids in the old city fabric of the French Concession, accessible only by ladder. Although cared for, they are "parked" here and generally do not leave. This symbolic congruence of cheap space and devalued personhood is particularly alarming.

In these cases, the broader city internalizes the economic logic of rentier architectures—retail, hotels and convention halls—which are always-already partially dead.

These do not expect thorough inhabitation, as in domestic architectures. Instead, their profit model works on the arbitrage of differentially productive assets, rooms and spaces. Empty rooms are offset by the returns on rented ones. This is the highly temporal architecture of occupancy rates, in which times of low demand are met with strategic devaluation. This leads to other interesting manifestations of the heterotopic interior, such as mega-churches that take advantage of cheap weekend rates for their Sunday services. We see this at Singapore's Suntec City and Expo Centre, where convention functions are mixed with big-box "revival" and Christian spectacle during off-peak hours. Since 2010, Suntec has been partially owned by an evangelical holding company.[8]

An introduction to partially dead typologies should also properly include a brief description of the taxidermic. In this phenomenon, the preserved corpse of a structure is preserved in state as an urban fragment, or more disturbingly as a false front for something new. The latter is analogous to the wearing of a skin for ornamental purposes, or as camouflage. The urban ruin becomes like a ceremonial hide, or the suit stitched by Buffalo Bill in *The Silence of the Lambs* (1991). This is a commonplace of heritage conservation, where the remains of non-viable buildings are stretched across the surfaces of newer and larger assemblies. In particular, one finds this technique employed in giving "character" to waterfront developments and post-industrial districts. This was the case with the failed Davol Square Marketplace (1982) in Providence, Rhode Island. Buildings along the Suzhou Creek in Shanghai follow the same model. Likewise the old "go-downs" that line the Singapore River, where the corpse is inhabited, somewhat like a pair of pants, by taller commercial structures. In reality, such artifacts may not be genuine; fake taxidermy is an amazing fact of contemporary architecture. It is a poignant irony of malls such as Providence Place in Rhode Island (1990), and Cambridgeside Galleria (1990) in Massachusetts, that they fabricate artificial post-industrial environments. That is, these construct new abandoned factories to inhabit—an appropriate, if depressing, optic for the magic of post-productive America, in which economic failure is repackaged as a marketable product.

It is an interesting post-note that dead spaces have also been a site of some imaginative investment, which converts their negativity into a form of life. This is especially the case with the revivifying architectural art of Takashi Kuribayashi, who fills necrotic voids with plants, water, and light. In a poignant moment, sequestered spaces, as well as the poché-world of suspended ceiling and flimsy partition, are transformed into miniaturized landscapes. Kuribayashi inserts into his limen-scapes poetic beings, seals and manatees, as well as plants, "rivers," stones and fallen logs. Just as amphibeans are able to move between environmental worlds, through water and land, earth and air, they likewise—in Kuribayashi's redemptive imaginary—become blithe spirits with the agility to trespass across the lively and morbid economies of the late modern building.

Reiteration and reflexivity

The reiterative is an odd kind of deviance. It is defined by replication, as well as in some cases by changes in scale. Although structured by common principles, the products of reiteration tend to be unpredictable. One instance might appear *osmotic*, like a clone emerging from a host. Another may be *fractal or kaleidoscopic*, with recognizable fragments—assemblies of limbs, or constellations of features—multiplying wildly. Much depends upon whether reiterated elements are complete or fragmentary, mature or juvenile, identical or distorted.

This is perhaps most clearly visible in botanical examples. In fact, the term "reiteration" is used by horticulturists to describe how a plant, under conditions of environmental stress, will attempt to grow itself anew at its own periphery. It will try to survive via replication, using its own tissue as a planting bed in lieu of soil. For example, a tree suffering compression of its roots will often produce stems called "water shoots." The latter exhibit a clear signature amid the normal branching of the tree, being rigidly vertical—they appear like flares, signaling the presence of an emergency. Water shoots look very much like saplings, sprouting upward from the existing limbs. And this is precisely what they are: the moribund tree is making a last-ditch attempt to transport its genetic self away from danger.

1. Danny Choo, "Separated at Birth," figurine series   2. Monozygotic twins, or "fetiform teratoma"   3. "Water shoots" in a damaged tree

1

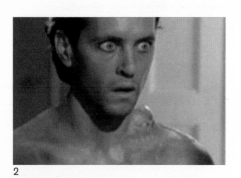

2

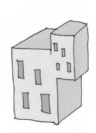

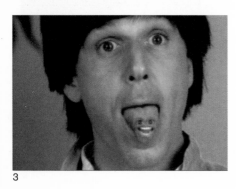

3

4

1. "Four-headed" frog found in UK, 2004   2. Still from *How to Get Ahead in Advertising*   3. Still from *Kung Pow: Enter the Fist*
4 "Osmotic" versus "fractal" reiteration

This same logic, applied to human anatomy, has produced a unique trope of bodily horror. Graphic images exist, for example, in Bruce Robinson's *How to Get Ahead in Advertising* (1989), and Sam Raimi's *Army of Darkness* (1992). In the former, a new head grows from the neck-pimple of copywriter Dennis Bagley. This tumescence turns out to be a ruthlessly effective Thatcherite executive, and the original Bagley begins to wither away. In Raimi's film, antihero Ash undergoes a similarly painful osmosis, as an evil *döppelganger* emerges from his shoulder. Osmotic reiteration appears in both cases as a shocking perversion of birth. Firstly, the new self is inappropriately identical to the original. Secondly, the procreative act does not take place in an organ that is prepared for it, but rather at an arbitrary rupture of the dermis. Thirdly, the new being arrives in some sense fully formed, with coordination and sophisticated malice. Here, osmosis is applied to creatures that do not reproduce in such a way, and the contrast is horrible.

In fact, the vegetable kingdom abounds with reiterative strategies of this kind, such as root-suckering and multi-stemmed growth. It is common to observe trees that appear as a tangle of conjoined clones, especially after damage. The arboricultural technique of "pollarding" makes use of this tendency. Principal branches are bluntly cut, and the tree responds by sending up clusters of water shoots at the stumps. The crown regrows fuller and faster, in a kind of Nietzschean pruning. A less controlled life-struggle is seen in the wake of storms, lightning strikes, or uncontrolled browsing by animals. In the sprouting of clones, a single specimen often appears at differing scales and stages of life, merged in a multiple exposure.

1. Stave churches, Norway 2. Bernd and Hilla Becher,
Grain Elevators, Ohio 3. Michelangelo, Medici Chapel and
Tomb of Guiliano de' Medici, San Lorenzo, Florence

By contrast, *fractal or kaleidoscopic* reiteration more commonly resembles the normal branching of a healthy tree. Here again, similar forms are conjoined in varying distributions, albeit in a far more fragmentary manner. Again, what is normal for the vegetative is aberrant in the vertebrate. Rhizomatic structure is acutely weird in animals. This principle is clearly sensed in genetic glitches, such as the "multi-frog"—in which several heads are attached to a common body. The arrayed limbs of the goddess-incarnation Bhadrakali are a powerful symbolic example, as are the hundred arms of the Greek giant Hecatoncheires. Reflexivity does not simply mean profusion, however. Fractal reiteration may also involve the nesting of one particular anatomical component in a new location. The faces of Janus are a sinister paradigm. William S. Burrough's "Spare Ass Annie" has an extra orifice (that one) in her forehead. In a ridiculous variant, the central character of Bob Odenkirk's *Kung Pow: Enter the Fist* (2002), is host to a wise-cracking face on the end of his tongue—that is, his tongue has a tongue.[1] The *vagina dentata* likewise reiterates the mouth, but via a particularly alarming instance of what Paul Ricoeur has elsewhere referred to as "predication."[2]

The osmotic may thus be distinguished from the fractal. In the latter, a single feature can define the aberration: an eye in the middle of the brow, an arm in the thorax, etcetera. This is the misplacement of a corporate element, not a new body *in fetu* or in miniature. It may also involve mass replication, as in an ostentation of eyes, limbs, fingers, teeth, and the like. However, the osmotic and the fractal may form part of a common process. That is, the reiterative may begin from a single component and grow into a competing subjectivity. Dennis Bagley's zit, and the evil eye in *Army of Darkness*, quickly become heads, with the intention of completing a malignant *döppelganger*—this is where the reflexive overlaps with other horrible tropes, such as the double and the clone.

In other cases, the reflexive is very much its own problematic: a remarkable kind of repetition. It is unlike the conjoined twin, wherein two equal beings are forced into a contiguous relation. In the latter, horror stems precisely from the erstwhile individuality of the two constituents. The "Siamese" twin would seem able to function independently, if he were not so yoked. Reiteration more properly involves the superimposition of fragments or partial copies. While the host is reduplicated, the second "self" is imperfectly related. It is often shrunken or distorted, a kind of faulty or fearful symmetry. For example, the monozygotic twin— because it dies and ceases to grow—is a morbid converse of the water shoot. Here, the body does not become reflexive in the struggle for life; the struggle has already been lost. The engaged corpse of the non-viable twin is the evidence of this uterine Cain-and-Abel drama.

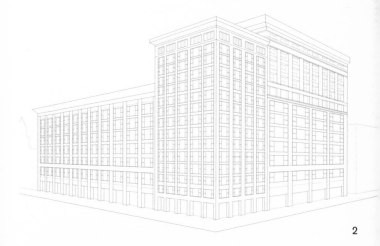

1. Holabird and Roche, Boston Department Store, Chicago, c. 1916
2. Boston Store, after a postcard c.1912; the height of the corner block
(what was formerly the Champlain Building) appears to be incorrect

In its play of repetition and scale, the category of the reflexive might also be thought to include the homunculus. But here again, some precision is needed. Reiteration is highly specific: a particular individual, or part thereof, is repeated. In most cases, the new element remains attached to its host. By contrast, the familiar, the troll or the tokoloshe occupies an independent body. Moreover, these need not replicate a person—only a type. The homunculus is, in this sense, a much more Platonic concept, in which the tiny being imperfectly mimics an ideal. Priapus likewise mirrors man, but less Platonically: his body and his genitals are at two different scales. What is being distorted here is not a man, but manhood generally.

In architecture, the unique character of reiteration becomes apparent when we consider some examples. One instance is the 1913 expansion of the Boston Department Store, in Chicago, by Holabird and Roche. As with many other deviants, this beautifully reflexive object grew from a purely commercial logic, as a casual byproduct of the expanding department store. The Boston was a voluminous establishment agglomerated in stages, a slow process of consumption that began from the original Champlain Building at the intersection of Madison and State in 1905, and spread north and west in phases. The original premises—seen at the corner in 1913—was massed as a tower. When read against the looming wings on either side, it provides a benchmark for the scalar explosion of the type. Later additions appear as a dramatically upscaled version of the original edifice. Note that the architects avoided any opportunity to ameliorate this disjunction. For example, they chose not to match any horizontal datum from the pioneering structure, which was stunted by the new standards of 1913 (and was demolished to make way for a new corner block a year later). No lines are continuous: no floor levels, no cornices, nothing. Even the portico at street level, and the entablature at its top, were enlarged in the later additions. The resulting effect is the appearance, in 1913, of two scales in a single building. One notes the fact that all phases employ a similar language, albeit differently sized; this emphasizes the abrupt disjuncture. As in a classic *mise-en-abyme*, the Boston store appears to replicate itself, and to shelter the wee double within its own body.

This is interesting if we recall the example of the water shoot. Like the tree, the Boston stands as an attempt to regrow itself. An identikit miniature appears to sprout from the tissue of the original. But in Holabird's building, the process is reversed: the dwarf version pre-dates the "proper" entity. The Boston is what the department store was eventually to become, and *not* the Champlain. Frozen in 1913, however, this phase in a progressive composition appears as a strikingly ambiguous and refractory take on the building as a singular object. Its "oneness" is a kind of Zen *koan*, a formal paradox. It is both one *and* more, a "whole" composition as well as an arrangement of differently scaled parts—which are, otherwise, nearly identical. This slippage defines the nature of the reiterative. It is an embryonic society of the self. In this way, the osmotic reiteration makes a muddle of the social. The self metastasizes to become self-and-other, "I-and-thou," parent and child. The Boston store is, in architectural terms, one hand clapping.

Of course, the architect of the Boston Store knowingly undertook no such project. Its reflexive narcissism is pre-post-modern, simply an outgrowth of the desire by the modern commercial enterprise to grow through progressive stages and iterations. Much like the analogous tree, the Boston store merely wished to continue being the Boston store, and—due to the nature of its industry, and to the expansive nature of character enterprises in a monopolistic moment—proliferation was crucial to its survival.

Again, these are *osmotic* examples of reiteration. Regardless of deviations, the tree and the building are replicated as largely "complete" entities. By contrast, in the *fractal or kaleidoscopic* version, a recognizable portion of the building—in effect, a thematic unit—is playfully repeated within the composition. This might be a shape, an assembly (such as an arrangement of windows) or an iconographic element. It is a technique that has often been used in the production of Mannerist and Postmodernist architectures.

The work of Michelangelo, for example, is full of reflexive moments. These have much to do with ludic disproportion, as seen in the Medici Chapel at San Lorenzo. Behind the sarcophagus of Guliano de' Medici, orders of two scales are nested. Great pilasters frame the walls and support the vault. Within these are set a secondary façade in *pietra serena*, with another, redundant structural system: smaller paired pilasters, a sub-entablature and blind windows. These are tightly tucked between the larger elements. It is a telescoping in which the wall appears to contract and recede. As with many of Michelangelo's reiterations, the bay provides a frame, a representational space in which the involution may occur. The façades at the Campidoglio on Rome's Capitoline Hill are an equally subversive statement. Two different orders are interposed within a single system of trabeation that adorns the building. The façades are built of self-supporting masonry.

The pillars are largely ornamental, a fact that is emphasized in their absurd disposition. These occur in two alternating types—large engaged pilasters and smaller freestanding columns—which famously appear to support lintels of different heights. The former make the latter unnecessary. This deployment gives the elevation a very peculiar tension, as if it were pulling and pushing against itself. Again, Michelangelo's repetition involves a kind of mischievous double-exposure. The architect plays in the space between structure and its expression, producing a vortex of readings.

A similar taste for paradox is at work in 19 Bin Tong Park, a private home in Singapore. This building is hardly high Mannerism. It is more an instance of "Low PoMo," characterized by a slightly hokey formal play around the repetition of the gable. The architect labors this joke heavily. The iconic form is exploited via a strategy of *antanaclasis*: it proliferates wildly, in each instance assuming a different connotation. Most obviously, the overall volume

Frank Gehry, ICA Building, New York

of the house is figured as an extruded gable; the part standing for the whole. This overarching envelope is then segmented into a number of imbricated gables of differing sizes and shapes. Gabled window pediments also intersect the house, perpendicularly. The shape is then deployed, yet again, in the production of decorative touches: pediments, triangular windows and glass-block openings in the perimeter wall. The architect's insistence on quotation is further weirded by the use of conflicting vocabularies. In some areas, for example, the roof is figured as an independent piece, while elsewhere it is bonded with the facade in a continuity of ceramic tile. Likewise, particular elements are ornamented, while others seem intentionally abstract. This would seem to be mere happenstance, if so many gestures in the design did not otherwise appear intentional.

19 Bin Tong Park might seem like an exuberant anomaly, an homage to Venturi or Stirling taken a little too far.[3] But interestingly, it is not the only example. A similarly

19 Bin Tong Park, Singapore

telescopic, reiterative hip roof is found not far away, in the James Tan Animal Clinic on Whitley Road. This example is rather more conservative, allowing itself less latitude of both form and material. Regardless, the architect interpolates the roof in order to produce a telescoping effect, in which the gable-end appears to contract. The building is, again, scaled and repeatedly inter-posited.

An excess of reflexivity, put to ambiguous ends, marks both buildings. In their self-referentiality and re-cycling of themes, they present a jejeune and excessive version of the modernist artistic product. In contrast to the controlled reflexivity of a Villa Savoie, for example, Bin Tong Park speaks in garbled—or gabled—quotations. This element becomes a mixed metaphor, hyper-extended and over-involved. It is literal *and* iconographic, tectonic *and* decorative. The hip roof is at once itself, a representation of itself, and the house entire. By contrast, biophysical reiteration tends toward clarity. The multi-frog is obviously a series of anura unhappily intersected, a zoomorphic stutter.

This begs the question of possibilities. What architectural freedoms are offered via the reflexive? What is interesting about osmotic reiteration is, in part, its imperfection: like Theseus's ship or Heraclitus' river, the original is never reconstituted exactly. It remains both the same *and* different. While the water shoot is a clone—the same genetic individual—it shadows its progenitor within a certain range of deviance, a margin of error. The new tree has a similar habit, as well as bark and foliage, flower and fruit. But it will not exactly replicate the original. The Boston store closely shadows the Champlain, but with some interesting deviations of vocabulary. This is a source of some creative possibilities. The reflexive monstrosity does not simply incubate an identical version at its perimeter. Rather, it produces a conjoined being that is ambiguous with respect to its independence.

Osmotic reflexivity thus introduces a fundamental break with architectural tradition: the freedom of the building not to be conceived as an object, but rather as a juxtaposition of versions. Its beauty involves seeing the same form, in multiple instances. This defies the notion of the conclusive product, and in so doing subverts one of the central assumptions of design. Instead, this strategy treats the reiterated morpheme as *something between form and type*. It assumes the character of a trope, a composition attempted through multiple iterations. In this process, the specific character of the work is subverted, and it begins to take on the heightened aspect of the general. Each version appears as an imperfect and conditional attempt at a transcendent ideal. The latter, rather romantically, is never fully realized.

Such an effect is central to architectures that draw their aesthetic charge from imperfect repetition. Many of Frank Gehry's later projects, post-Vitra, employ this technique. His ICA building in New York, for example, derives much of its beauty from the variability of its prows—curvatures which, it must be said, would border on trite if any were to be treated as the singular or conclusive version. A number of Bilbao-era projects similarly superimpose many variants of a common element. Peter Eisenman's Church of the Year 2000 in Rome, and his Emory Center For the Arts (1991), suggest a more calculated version. Other examples of this technique include Oosterhuis Associates' Dancing Façades, in Groningen (1995);[4] J.L.

Esteban Penelas' Sanchez-Mendez House project for Madrid (2003);[5] and MVRDV's Donau City competition for Vienna (2002).

The apparent casualness of this technique conceals its power. Osmotic reiteration, in particular, offers something more than the kaleidoscopic distributions of Postmodernism or parametric architecture. Its emphasis is less upon the play of icons, as in the former. Or, in the building made from scripts, upon the minor degrees of freedom exerted by elements *en masse*. Particularly in the latter, the singularity of the object remains dominant— the "swarm" is, in spite of its roiling, a unitary thing. Multiplicity is, here, a kind of superficial or ornamental effect. This is not true of the water shoot or the interrupted act of osmosis, which instead emphasizes the genuine possibility of the single work of architecture as (again) a kind of awkward social being. Reiteration proposes a transformational play of multiples, an undefined and largely unexplored midpoint between architecture and urbanization, individual and species.

Incontinent Object

Speech, consumption and excretion are acts that connect the social world to an otherwise inscrutable interior. For this reason, in part, we monitor orifices closely. We like to know where they are and what they will do.

The relative predictability of the orifice is contrasted, in horror, with *holes*. The latter are unexpected perforations of the body's external membrane, and unsurprisingly, there is some discomfort associated with them. These are disturbing by degrees. Cuts and abrasions are certainly unwelcome. Gaping voids are worse (see Partially Dead). But especially revolting is the appearance of a functionally-specific aperture. Such is the case, for example, in Charles Burns' *Black Hole*, when a virus causes a teenager to grow a mouth on his chest.[1] Or in Sam Raimi's *Army of Darkness*, when a socket opens in the shoulder blade of the protagonist, and an eye begins to look about.

The hole suggests an inability to enforce the order or territoriality of the body. It may operate independently of the will of its host—performing strange functions, allowing traffic in or out.[2] The breach is a threshold of momentous, and possibly dangerous, agency. Aleksandar Hemon captured this in his description of Archduke Ferdinand, staring into the sphincter of an imperial horse at the moment of his assassination:

> the horse on the left raises its
> tail—embarrassingly similar to the
> tassel on Archduke's resplendent
> helmet—and the Archduke can see
> the horse's anus slowly opening,
> like a camera aperture.[3]

Of course, what is about to be birthed from this *anus horribilis* is the 20th century itself, with the cataclysmic founding violence of the Great War. This dilation opens a rift in the fabric of history.

As the hole opens where it should not, the incontinent object releases that which should be kept inside. It is a form of physical deviance in which bodies resist enclosure. The interior refuses to remain so; those elements that should rightly be hidden burst into public.

Factory shed, Jurong, Singapore

(above) Wiring in a collectivized house, Shanghai
(below) Still from John Carpenter's *The Thing*

Façade accretions, Shanghai

1. Ducting reclaimed during demolition, Shanghai   2. Bernd and Hilla Becher, Blast Furnace, Cleveland, Ohio, 1980

3. Extraction ducting and chimney stack, restaurant, Shanghai
4. Renzo Piano and Richard Rogers, Pompidou Centre, Paris

Incontinence emerges here in two major variants: herniation and pollution. These incorporate ideas of putrefaction, expulsion, and contagion—but also enchantment and power. All are part of a common horror. Numerous examples exist in the broader culture, and in the mythosphere: from the Scylla of the Greeks, to ghosts and poltergeists, to the cursed De La Poer family of Lovecraft's *The Drowned*. In the recent Japanese genre of "tentacle porn," an opening in the skin may erupt into a bolus of articulate viscera. This trope is present, also, in popular imaginaries of magic and witchcraft, as well as in the fear of the contagious outsider, the plague-bringer, and the irradiated subject.

In certain respects, this is a modern nightmare. As Lewis Mumford, Michel Foucault, and others have pointed out, it was only recently that continence was expected of people, buildings, and cities.[1] Not so long ago, all was—to a degree—porous. In an age of humoral medicine, bodies were understood to be radiant, and susceptible, beyond the limit of their dermal horizons. Such an assumption fueled the belief in phlogiston, a combustible essence presumed to grow from the metabolism. This was thought to rise above the shoulders in a coniform taper, like a hood. Melville's Ishmael described it, in *Moby-Dick*, as "a curious involved worming and undulation in the atmosphere over my head."[2] Likewise, Victorians presumed "animal magnetism" to be a a medium of influence, a social electricity. In 19th-century Britain, W.J. Vernon and other Mesmerists staged an invasion of the will by means of this intimate conductivity.[3] Individuals, under the persuasion of another's penetrating current, were made to follow commands and exhibit unorthodox behaviors.

But assumptions of human sensitive interaction—for example, of the brain and blood as parts of a "galvanic battery"—were increasingly under attack.[4] In the conception of new clinical science, humans were re-fashioned (in Louis Althusser's term, "interpolated") as contained subjects with unseemly interiors.[5] Lewis Mumford noted that each came to be emptied, bathed, and sexed in a regime of what he called "Baroque regularity." This may be polemical overstatement, but historians of science observe that the development of tissural medicine reinforced a conception of the person as increasingly hermetic, and bounded.

Buildings were subjected to a similar process. Prior to the internalization of plumbing, human waste was evident and available, a fixture of the public sphere. It lay at the road in open drains, or was unceremoniously ejected from windows. The builders of the eighteenth century devised means of enclosing effluents, sequestering bodily functions and hiding their evidence.[6] Cloacina, the goddess of Rome's main sewer, was—after nearly two millennia of inactivity—once more ascendant. Cities were "cloacinated," their drains enclosed. Shortly after, they were also electrified, and linked through the attenuations of telephony. The interior was sewn with ducts, wires, and cables. The order of pre-modern urban building was turned inside out. Or rather, it was turned outside-in.[7]

Modern buildings, like modern subjects, thus came to contain unspeakable cavities. Channeled winds, mobile waste, captive lightning—all of these are smuggled into the walls of the home and the office. Those who work in design and construction are familiar with these obscure and recessive spaces, how they contradict the resolved

bourgeois exterior. Simply put, they are a mess. In order to sustain this disappearing act, the modern partition is conceived as a complex assembly of membranes, organized around a vacancy. Again, this is quite recent. The walls of the pre-modern building had no unseemly interior. Their poché was merely mass that simulated the geological.

In the modern era, "better" architectures have generally been more successful in their attempt to hide this dark matter. But it has everywhere given rise to a crisis of concealment. The pellucid design strategies of Modernism—what Colin Rowe and Robert Slutzky called its "literal and phenomenal" transparency—have consistently failed to meet the challenge of plumbing.[8] Like the psychoanalytic subject, the modern building has frequently been unable to assimilate its revolting technical interior.

The crisis of concealment resulted in many solutions, two more common than the others. One is the Functionalist exposure of working elements. This was a common area of experiment in the famous Case Study Houses of the 1940s and 1950s, and will be familiar to anyone who has inhabited the stylistic space of the "post-industrial." This approach veered into more anarchic expressions in the 1960s and 1970s, in the interiors of Joe Colombo, Verner Panton, and Team X. True to the culture of the Archigram moment, the errant duct here assumed a ludic, loopy, hippy aspect. But more frequently, its contents were remanded to the rarely-accessed "chases" that vein the modern structure. Such unmentionables have rarely been confidently aired in public. For this reason, the inversion of Renzo Piano and Richard Roger's Pompidou Centre still has a vaguely transgressive and scatological atmosphere about it—evoking Bunuel's *Discreet Charm of the Bourgeoisie* (1972), in which characters sit side-by-side on the toilet.

A second, contrasting strategy was that of disappearance. This was the illusion that the building need no services whatsoever. Mies' Barcelona Pavilion (1929) is perhaps the clearest expression of such a fantasy. Mechanical systems seem to have vanished. Even structure has become attenuated. The steel columns appear to be in tension, as if straining to keep the roof from floating away. The notion of function is dissolved in a planar abstraction, a vagueness structured by formal precision. This is the realm of ideas. Ducting would imply embarrassing physicality, out of place in such a rarefied aether. The same is true of the glass box, which would appear to hide nothing so literal as a pipe— despite longstanding ideological links between utopia and plumbing.[9] One must suspend disbelief when looking at the John Lautner houses, perched like aeries at an altitude above hygiene. For we know that, without fail, plumbing has been banished to some dusty cabinet within.

Mies' vanishing-act continued in the best of Skidmore, Owings and Merrill's projects from mid-century, and in particular under Gordon Bunschaft. At the same time, a clarified relation of service and "served" spaces was also famously pursued by Louis Kahn, who rued "the burying of tortured, unwanted ducts."[10] In particular at the Kimbell Art Museum (1972), where, the Miesian system—in effect, a shell-game of stuffing and hiding—was rejected in favor of a rationalized role for HVAC and "wet" elements within the modernist tectonic.

For less technically accomplished architects, however, the strategy of concealment was a doomed enterprise. A nightmare of modern building has been the failure to contain this complexity. Public housing and sprawling institutional edifices are often marked by a proliferation of "guts." Badly resolved concrete structures, in particular—where care must be taken in passing mechanical and electrical services across the beams—fall victim to the varicoceles of PVC piping, foil ducting and the trunking of electrical wires. This was archly visualized in Lars von Trier's *The Kingdom* (1994), in which a hospital lauded as a triumph of architectural rationalism begins to sink within an ancient bog. The latter invades the building and produces a shameful recrudescence of the pre-modern: failing services, ghosts, cult activity, and the like. Toby Litt's novel *Hospital* presents an even more extravagant vision, in which the building itself is an immense and straining body, with mucosal surfaces, villi, muscles and fibers. Likewise, Terry Gilliam's *Brazil* (1985) envisioned a failure to conceal the spasmodic viscera behind well-composed, but paper-thin, authoritarian surfaces. The tubes continually burst forth from behind their partitions and homasote ceilings, a sort of architectural hernia that airs the scandal of the interior. The opening line of Gilliam's film, "let's talk about ducts," has a slightly obscene, as well as clinical, ring to it.

Herniated objects are thus the accidental products of modernism's constructive mythologies: lightness, abstraction, minima, and transparency. They are likewise the victims of its injurious capacities. This is clearest, perhaps, in the cataclysmic sacking of cities such as Hiroshima and Nagasaki, Rotterdam and fire-bombed Dresden. But punctured urban fabric is similarly the result of "creative destruction:" the revolutions of un- and re-making unleashed by capital processes. This can be seen, hyperbolically, in contemporary Shanghai and Beijing, where the old domestic structures of "lane houses" (*nongtang* and *hutong*) are sacrificed to make way for new ventures. With the removal of façades, rooms are suddenly opened to the street, vented with their personal trappings still inside. Wallpaper and photographs remain tacked to the wall; laundry hangs in midair, above floors since hammered away. As materials from demolition are often harvested and cycled into subsequent construction, it is not uncommon to stumble upon great tangles of disemboweled ducting, coiled and waiting to be transplanted elsewhere. The deconstruction can seem slow and surgical. Often, frontages alone are removed, as if split along some invisible meridian and peeled away. The dwelling is opened like a dollhouse. Nancy Munn has written of similar phenomenal unease in the 19th-century transformation of New York, and in particular those houses that were slowly de-laminated during the construction of Central Park. Edgar Allan Poe, among others, noted the melancholy of this forensic strip-tease.

In such cases, one is presented with a vivisection, a flaying. The building is alive, and is inappropriately opened.[11] As we have argued, the hernia is likewise alarming as a failure of abstraction, a moment in which the corporeal program of modernism is unequal to the complexity of contemporary buildings. These are jarring, to be sure, but they hardly exhaust the trope of incontinence.[12] There is a more vaporous, but no less sinister, variant of the body's breach: the entity that emanates influences beyond its envelope. This is the radiant being, the "sick" building. Not herniation, that is, but pollution.

There are many literary and popular variants of such miasmic architecture. As discussed above (see Partially Dead), narratives of urban haunting draw heavily upon the idea of contagion, and upon the assumed communicability of death and traumatic history. Points of contact with the spectral realm—haunted houses, shrines, and cemeteries—are nearly universally associated with a risk of possession, sickness, and tragedy. Sites of violence and perversion are to be avoided for the same reason. Poe's House of Usher, for one example, is defined by this imaginary. It is a building that gives material expression to a moral degeneracy: in particular, the unseemly intimacy between Roderick Usher and his sister. The manor stands over a bog, into which it eventually subsides. This is a landscape of incest, stagnant and recursive, which appropriately collapses into itself. The decay of the edifice and of its lineage gives rise to a peculiar "atmosphere," which the narrator believes "had no affinity with the air of heaven, but which had reeked up from the decayed trees, and the gray wall, and the silent tarn—a pestilent and mystic vapour."[13] The dissolution of Usher's line through endogamous union, and the burial of the still-living sister within the family crypt, result in a cataclysmic "reverberation." It is a final throb of negation with a radiance like that of the "blood-red moon," that tears the house to pieces.[14]

Similar emanations occur in a number of Rudyard Kipling's stories, including "They" and "The House Surgeon." In the former, Kipling's narrator is drawn by the ghosts of children to an obscure manor in the country, as if his car "took the road of her own volition."[15] The occupant, a blind spinster, confesses to have lured the spirits out of a selfish desire for their company, as one who has "neither born nor lost." One of these ghosts—who, it is implied, may be the narrator's own—draws him to the estate from "across the country," and tenderly kisses his hand by the fire. This odd house channels the yearning scars of infant mortality into a sort of magnetism. By contrast, "The House Surgeon" describes not an attraction but a repulsion. The focus of this tale is also a home, purchased by a family without knowledge of its history. The narrator is called to verify a peculiar effect, in which inhabitants are plunged into an unbearable dread, a "depression," lasting for intermittent periods. Experiencing the onset of this effect, the visitor recalls that:

> my brain telegraphed that it was the forerunner of a swift-striding gloom... despair upon despair, misery upon misery, fear upon fear, each causing their distinct and separate woe, packed in upon me for an unrecorded length of time.[16]

Frank Relle, Choctau, from *New Orleans Nightscapes*, 2010

In a familiar trope of the horror genre, this torment is the reverberation of mis-acknowledged tragedy: a woman who was wrongly assumed to have committed suicide by falling from the window.

Spiritual malaise—horror and melancholy, lunacy and listlessness—transmits at Gothic frequencies. Its infectious character is a cliché of fantastic and romantic fiction. But pollution can be more literal. The architectures of industrial disaster provide real examples. Such is the case with failed nuclear facilities, and the relics of Cold War atomic programs. Chernobyl is the ur-example of the invisibility of radiant threat. The frightening mobility of the cloud, of plutonium and other fission compounds, led analysts such as Ulrich Beck to announce an age in which risk was truly post-territorial.[17] The *Ka'aba*-like image of the reactor core cast in its concrete "sarcophagus" provided a suitably terrifying centroid to the disaster, at once abstract and uncannily solid: the voiding of a void, the final removal from inhabitability of a piece of the earth's surface. Likewise the abandonment of a 30-kilometer "Zone of Alienation"[18] around the town of Pripyat suggested a negativity to complement the entombed mass. Photographs of this post-human landscape, largely abandoned since 1986, suggest a nature fundamentally altered. Alan Weisman has chronicled such cases, in which anthropogenic environments are suddenly depopulated. The result appears somehow traumatized, or unconvincingly "natural." The strange powers that hold sway here are announced by silence, and by emptiness.

This charged quietude indicates the unseen presence of an unwelcome influence. A John Cage-like atmosphere surrounds the object-relics of other toxic sites, also. These include the cooling towers of Three Mile Island, near Harrisburg, Pennsylvania. Likewise, the barren platforms of earth in the former town of Uravan, Colorado, completely dismantled at the conclusion of plutonium-mining operations. Or the fragments of road cross-cutting Centralia, Pennsylvania, where fires in a network of coal mines have created a vulcan landscape of potholes, carbon dioxide vents, and 1,000-degree subterranean furnaces. Perhaps the most discomfiting example is the ruin of Union Carbide's facility at Bhopal, where the exhalation of toxic gasses led to the deaths of 3,787 people. Kai Ericsson has analyzed this terminal silence—and the shock of revelation—in his psychological study of polluted communities. In particular, Ericsson records the response of families to the realization that their neighborhoods have been progressively undermined by silent seepages that threaten their health and devalue their homes. Similar issues surround "cancer clusters" at electrical pylons, telephone interchanges, and factories.

Vaporous influences can be less malignant, if still insidious. In the 1980s, for example, designers from the office of John Portman floated the notion of "teaser air:" wisps of cool escaping from the air-conditioned interior were to be used to lure the public inside, taking advantage of hot climates such as Atlanta and Singapore. The timing of sliding doors, and the functioning of the thermal breaks called "air curtains," were calibrated to leak. Beyond the structure was a larger, invisible circumference: a cumulus of comfort to grab the overheated consumer. Portman's innovation was part of a contemporaneous trend in the micro-engineering of sensation, particularly in the

design development of places like Las Vegas. The same
evolution gave rise to scented air—evoking baking food,
or human pheromones—that is used to spur impulsive
buying in retail environments, and to draw visitors across
the threshold. Companies such as International Flavors and
Fragrances (IFF) and Givaudin have developed a technical
specialty in such rarefied atmospherics, a super-engineered
flatulence. Expensively "conditioned" air forms a sort *ignis
fatuus*: that cold and strangely charged vapor that escapes
from the grave and inflames the imagination.

The many varieties of spiritual and industrial
pollution recall monstrous figures from supernatural fictions,
those who exercise power at a distance. The magician or
enchanter is a clear archetype: Prospero, Merlin, Voldemort.
The conflation of dominance and toxicity recalls the
villain of Somerset Maugham's *The Magician*. Or, in a more
redemptive guise, the trickster Conchis of John Fowles'
The Magus. Likewise, we might consider sirens, telekinetics
and mutants, cultists and satanists. The monster is often
identified with a penumbra of power; he carries with him
a sphere of influence. In the case of Melville's *Moby-Dick*,
this is described as a sort of anti-halo. His Ishmael notes:

> how nobly it raises our conceit of the
> mighty, misty monster, to behold him
> solemnly sailing through a calm tropical
> sea; his vast, mild head overhung by a
> canopy of vapor...as if Heaven itself had
> put its seal upon his thoughts.[19]

The demon radiates a kind of ungovernable force, or a
messianic intensity, which results in a derangement
of the atmosphere. The figure of the witch, far from

extinct, continues to embody this sort of power in many contemporary contexts. The recent transition to a "globalized" economic footing, in particular, has brought with it renewed allegations of witchcraft, as well as killings of its alleged practitioners. The modernity of this practice has been demonstrated in Cameroon by Peter Geschiere, in Indonesia by James Siegel, and in South Africa by Jean and John Comaroff. Likewise, Michael Taussig has described the belief in satanic moneys and commodities in Latin America.

In a political analogue, remote control is often manifest in the architecture of the dictator or autocrat.[20] This was the case with Idi Amin, Saddam Hussein and Joseph Mobutu, as well as Hitler, Mussolini, and Stalin. Such enchanters often make use of intelligence networks, but also television, radio, and other modes of mass communication. This is captured in the spectral appearances of Papa Doc Duvalier's Tonton Macoute in Graham Greene's *The Comedians.* Horrid buildings often serve as symbolic centers of such coercion: the headquarters of the East German Stasi network, Burma's Insein Prison, or the stadium (with torture chambers below) that was the center of Mobutu's entropic regime. The character of these structures is perhaps best figured in George Orwell's Ministry of Love: a windowless box and panoptical center, from which the techniques of mass cooptation are deployed.

Again, the aesthetics of the polluting or controlling monstrosity engage the image of the object and its "radius"—the thing and its undetectable, expansive penumbra. The object appears to compose the landscape around itself. The sarcophagus, cooling tower or authoritarian bunker comes to act as a vanishing point;

everything nearby appears to refer to it.

One is correct to fear this building that radiates, vomits, or spreads its lamina in public space. It undermines that beloved conceit, the sovereignty of the individual. The incontinent building is excessively sociable. As Wells Tower has written of the "flayed house," of New Orleans or Detroit, "you feel the sordid burden of unsolicited intimacy."[21] It is prone to neurotic confession, to the blurting of embarrassing secrets. By contrast, the idealized modern megalith stands mute and autonomous, like a Hugh Ferris silhouette: Olympus above the urban canyon. Ayn Rand would find the contrast contemptible. Atlas shrugs; he never farts.[22]

This shameful gesture likewise speaks a disconcerting truth about power itself. The latter always-already operates at a distance. The herniating or radiant horror asserts that the subject does not coincide with his anatomical limits: that humans continue to exert, and remain susceptible to, forms of influence that extend beyond themselves. Indeed, its lesson holds that power resists resolution into bodies, buildings, and other territorial envelopes. The failure of bounded entities—humans, states, institutions—figure centrally in this imaginary.

Trojan Horse

The "doubling" or multiplicity of the monstrous building may take other forms besides adjacency. The semi-detached home provides an archetype for the latter, as we have seen. A less obvious, but perhaps equally disconcerting, form of duality might be called the Trojan Horse. In this case, a dissociation or rift occurs between the contents of a building and its expression. Like the components of an exquisite corpse, the inside and outside do not match. There remains a creepy, sometimes malevolent, interiority.

This is an old standby of science and horror fiction, in which the human form is inhabited by something alien. "Bodysnatchers" are a famous example. The Trojan Horse is any being or object that is not what it would seem. As such, this category comprises the confidence man, the quack, the spy, and the mole. It would also include malevolent spirits that take possession of vulnerable individuals—such as "Captain Howdy" in *The Exorcist* (1973), whose behavior contrasts so horrifyingly with the vehicle of a young girl. This interloper who would wear the body as a "mask" or costume expresses the fundamental principle of Freud's *unheimlich*: the conflation of that which is intimate and that which is foreign in the same entity.

The Trojan Horse likewise includes the "psycho." The latter may be a person who conceals ill intent beneath a mask of normalcy, like Bret Easton Ellis' Patrick Bateman.

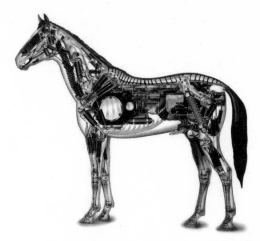

1. George Ladas, Robotic Horse Techincal Cutaway   2. Haniffa
Tower Home, Singapore   3. Tianzi Hotel, Hebei Province, PRC

1

2

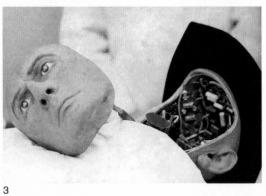

3

More dramatically, their body might house an additional personality—a second self—that creeps among the detritus of the fractured or fragmented individual. The mismatch of appearances becomes yet more chilling when the invader contradicts the host in terms of gender or age. This is most iconically the case with Alfred Hitchcock's Norman Bates, who "doubles" as his dead mother.

Architecturally, this sort of aberration emerges (again) at the interface of new typology and old language. An apt historical example is the neoclassical theater or opera house, which introduced technical requirements not easily integrated into rational envelopes. At least, these were not assimilable into enclosures where the interior and exterior assume common forms. This is partly because the modern theater is an unprecedentedly large and peculiar volume of space, in effect a "bubble." Of course, a number of Baroque buildings, such as Borromini's Oratorio dei Filippini (1637–50), incorporated sizable voids. This occurred long before the urbanization of opera in the 18th and 19th centuries.[1] However, the scale of the new theaters exceeded, in plan if not section, the great rooms that had gone before—due in part to the long-span possibilities of iron structure, and the burgeoning size of bourgeois audiences.

More problematic, perhaps, is the modern auditorium's complex sequence of volumes, each distinct with respect to its neighbor. One can see the results, for example, in the longitudinal section of Charles Garnier's Paris Opera (1875). In an attempt to rationalize the massing according to classical principles of composition, the architect is forced to disarticulate interior and exterior. The domes and vaults are not legible from without; rather, these are hidden beneath what is, in effect, a shed roof.

1. Eric Tabuchi, from the series *Eldorado,* 2009 2. Jed Caesar, *Geode*, 2004   3. Robot effect from the film *Westworld*, 1973

As Robert Venturi and Denise Scott Brown observed in *Complexity and Contradiction*, an odd zone emerges between these two dermal layers, a kind of expanded poché. Even more interesting, the "loose skin" at the exterior may often be developed as an independent ornamental and iconographic program.[2] Inner and outer surfaces are synchronized principally at openings, such as the great entry ways and windows. Elsewhere, their elaborations proceed with a casual disregard for one another. A technical "goo" of structure and services insulates the inhabitable spaces from the envelope.

This would contrast with Trajan's Baths (104-9 AD), for example. In the latter, the sequence of whole and half-domes is expressed in the roof-line of the building. Likewise, in the Serapeum of Hadrian's Villa (c. 130 AD). This is not to argue that classicism obliged an "honest" or transparent relationship between interior volumes and their exterior expression. Quite the contrary. Renaissance architects, in particular, cultivated a fascinating ambiguity on the subject. Their designs for exterior envelopes frequently employed symmetrical compositions—including regularly arrayed elements, windows and ornaments—which belied complex and asymmetrical distributions of rooms at the interior. As shown by Preston Scott Cohen in his detailed analysis of the Church of Santa Teresa, the conflict of these systems often forced innovations in the resolution of windows and poché at the façade.[3] Moreover, the status of the special room, deeply buried in the plan, remained unresolved with respect to the exterior. Even in the rigorous Neoclassicism of Schindler, as in the Altes Museum (1830), the presence of a dome and drum at the heart of the plan is totally occluded at the façade.

However, if the pressures of the modern world did not give birth to the "dishonest" envelope, they certainly exacerbated it. The divorce of surface and depth continues to be driven by forces of consolidation and interiorization. Recent buildings have tended to enclose a welter of micro-environments, each with their own functions, atmospheric effects and contrivances. In short, their density and heterogeneity enforce a kind of Deleuzian schizophrenia: the "great indoors" becomes simply too complex to be expressed outwardly. Such a phenomenon is archly articulated in the speculative archeological artifacts of artist Jedediah Caesar. Works such as Geode (2004) present monolithic objects that are neither clearly geological, nor man-made. On closer inspection, they are composed of modern, anthropogenic detritus. This interior life is a surprise, as an encounter with the piece reveals it in increasing detail.

Interestingly, the large commercial building follows a similar formal logic. Such is the *mise-en-abyme* of Ikea, for example, where the studied abstraction of the blue box—an architectural equivalent of the unassuming psychotic—misrepresents the turmoil therein.[4] The commercial megastructure is a type with unique peculiarities. But the problem is no less applicable to the apartment block. In this quotidian (albeit bizarre) urban contraption, a single container must enclose a cosmos of interiorities. In light of such inner chaos, the externality of the building becomes arbitrary. At best, it is neutral; more commonly, it is subject to some kind of stylistic treatment. The block of flats, like the "big box," lacks an innate expression, and a result is the sort of thematic free-for-all seen in the early days of the high rise.

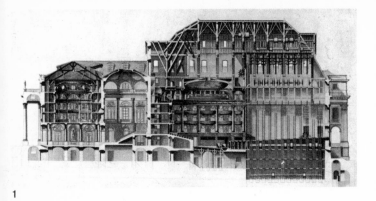

1

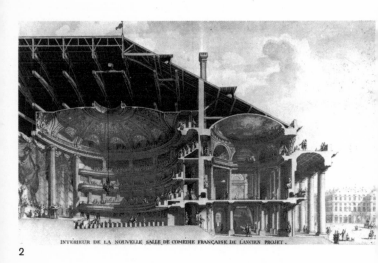

INTÉRIEUR DE LA NOUVELLE SALLE DE COMÉDIE FRANÇAISE DE L'ANCIEN PROJET.

2

1. Marie de Peyre and Charles de Wailly, Théâtre-Français, Paris
2. Victor Louis, Grand Théâtre, Bordeaux 3. Charles Garnier, Paris
Opera 4. Charles Francois Ribart, Triumphal elephant for Louis XV

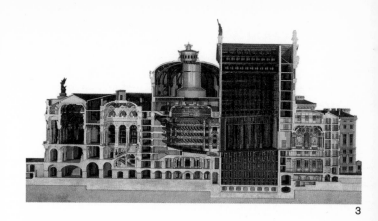

3

4

Thus a powerful source of schizophrenia is internalization itself: the mounting separation between private contents and the public sphere. As Robin Evans observed in his "Windows, Doors, and Passages," this is something that has occurred at all scales, and even within the relatively humble apartment or house.[5] Evans' point—argued also, by Hannah Arendt in *The Human Condition*—is that the inside has become more and more interior.[6] That is, the private appears to recede ever further from the public. At the same time, compartmentalization continues to subdivide the plan. As architects are aware, the contemporary urban apartment demonstrates the paradoxical effects of this process. While footages have decreased, rooms have become more numerous.

Such architectures reinforce the Victorian notion that the private space is, very profoundly, a world apart. Perhaps this is why Poe felt obliged to publish a "Philosophy of Furniture," in 1840. The freedom of the interior, especially when matched to the American liberty from aristocratic tastes, creates an acutely horrible condition. Poe understood that furnishing a room always entails a sort of existential crisis, as no rationality exists to guide it. Hence the author's own helpful, if sardonic, advice. Poe was also acutely aware of its Gothic intimacy: the strange experience of the visitor who surrenders himself to another's miniature kingdom. What sort of creepy potentials arise when the inside is, in a real sense, its own domain? Although perhaps less over-stuffed and over-decorated, it remains a site of intense signification: of class, taste, and other hallmarks of social identity. For this reason, the interior has become an increasingly urgent subject, and there remains something arbitrary and worrisome about it.

Designers have attempted to engage the specter of the idiosyncratic interior in a variety of ways. There is a strange "trickle down" effect at work here: it becomes not merely a problem of large architecture, but of architecture at large. The question asks to be addressed, as Poe saw, at the scale of the individual home. Adolf Loos recognized this also, and proposed perhaps the most convincing solution in the form of his Raumplan. One notes—particularly when looking at color photographs of Villa Müller (1928-30) and Khuner Country House (1929-30)—the degree of freedom allowed to the rooms. These are the principal organizing substance of the house, but each is given a life of its own: in its location in plan and section, in color, and in its character and program. The envelope and the rooms remain distinct with respect to one another. This gives rise to the famous muteness of the Loosian exterior, the lack of indications about what happens within. It is, in short, a Trojan Horse. Through his method, however, Loos found a compromise between unity and multiplicity. The house is profoundly defined by its spaces, peripatetic though these may be. The room makes good on the potentials of its unique freedom, without destroying the totality of the work.

By contrast, others have frankly embraced the arbitrariness of the interior, and moved toward an aggressively scenographic approach. The inside becomes a space of fantasy, in which the architect indulges. The interior is, quite literally, something "apart," and the normal strictures of design do not apply. One sees this clearly in a Smoking Room belonging to Frank Furness, which the architect built for himself at his home in Philadelphia (ca. 1880). Here, the urban context is eradicated completely—

the cabinet is like a folly. It presents itself as a rustic and rude hunting cottage, set (it would seem), impossibly far from the civilizing influences of New England. The design language of this can only be described as "itchy:" moth-eaten animal skins are piled in heaps, and one can vaguely perceive motes of dust swirling about in the air. The walls are roughly half-timbered, in a manner quite alien to Furness' famous masonry. It is manly, and unrelievedly horrid. Perhaps the architect was recreating a frontier outpost from his days as a Union soldier; or he may have been demonstrating just how far he was willing to go in the production of shock. The effect is present in certain interiors by Maybeck, also, at the University of California in Berkeley. His gymnasium and dining room at Hearst Hall (1899), for example, create their own peculiar stylistic language, a sort of West Coast medievalism. Lights hang from the ceiling like censers, and the athletic space in particular appears to have been intended for training students in the chivalric arts.

This theatrical tendency appears equally attractive to recent architects. It was certainly the preference of Verner Panton, who created internal environments that aggressively erased the world beyond. These tended to be womb-like, or perhaps intestinal, in an extreme version of the 1970s "rec room" aesthetic. The designer's family home in Binningen, Switzerland (ca. 1970), is reminiscent of the set for Roger Vadim's *Barbarella* (1968): swarms of fabric balls cascade from the ceiling; stalactites of glass, shell and mirror produce the impression of a crystal cave. Panton's "Visiona 2 Environment" for Bayer Fibres (1970) was similar, as was Ico Parisi's Lenno House on Lake Como (1978), and Yasutaka Yamazaki's Hall of Wedding

1. Verner Panton, Panton apartment, Binningen
2 Adolf Loos, Khuner House room, Payerbach

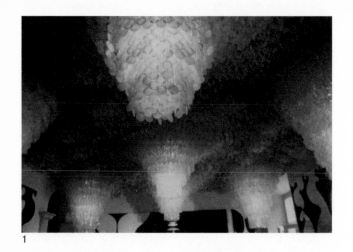

1

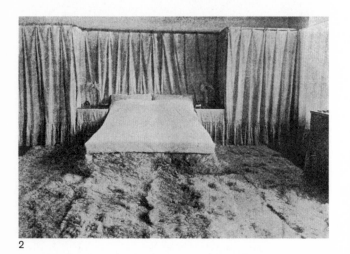

2

1. Verner Panton, Visiona 2 Environment, Bayer Fibres, Köln
2. Adolf Loos, Loos Apartment

Ceremonies in Nagoya (1975). The contemporary moment is conceptually, if not stylistically, kindred. At the Hotel Fox in Copenhagen (2005), for example, the designers embrace the somewhat terrifying notion that each of the guest quarters might be a complete thematic work unto itself, bearing no relation to its neighbors or to the larger container. The Fox, which was born as a marketing exercise for Volkswagen, is based on an assumption that "surprise" is a form of added value.[7] This same effect has been deployed somewhat differently in the hotels of Las Vegas, where the removal of external referents—be they social, temporal, or environmental—has been correlated to high gambling proceeds. The casinos thus work to eradicate any suggestion of a larger context, and mine the potentials of the thematic interior. This is reinforced via a lack of windows and clocks, and the creation of mediating zones that put maximum distance between access points and gaming halls.

This aggressive conceptual de-linking of inside and out is a strange aspect of the Trojan Horse. Another manifestation is a kind of "typological drift" in which the reading of buildings according to normative identifiers becomes muddled. Previously, one might have expected a consistent relationship between an historical type and its contents: for example, that a bank does not appear like a house, or vice versa. This is no longer a safe assumption. Shifts in program have been the result of cataclysmic event: of imperialism, military action or demographic change. This was the case, for example, with the eviction of Christians from the Hagia Sophia, which led to its transformation from church to mosque. The coastal defense structures of Fort Hero, New York were made to look like a Long Island Town from the air, in order to reduce the

1. Shoe House, Hellam, Pennsylvania   2. Cutaway view,
Mini Cooper   3. Fang Yuan Building, Shenyang, PRC

risk of their being bombed. In the same way, an Allied observation tower at the Atlantic Wall, documented by Paul Virilio, was camouflaged as a church belfry.[8] Such extreme circumstances might also include the radical devaluation of architectures, and their opportunistic reuse. This was the case of the former Michigan Theatre in Detroit, which now houses cars.

Less dramatic circumstances gave rise to the Haniffa Tower Home (2009), in Singapore, where a high-rise apartment block was built for a single family.[9] This is another case of increased consolidation: of the number of family members living under a common roof, certainly. But also of wealth, in which the magnitude of personal fortunes have caught up with typologies formerly considered too expensive for private monies. The spectacularity of this circumstance reached an apex with Antilia, a billion-dollar high-rise home built by petrochemical magnate Mukesh Ambani, in Mumbai, in 2010.

In modern architecture, confusion among typologies continues to arise from the failure to give them an independent expression. What, in the vocabulary of the International Style, marks a school—or even a large single-family house—as distinct from a museum? Or, again, a bank? All are subject to a universal design language. This failure likewise results from the myth of a transparent relationship between interior and exterior. Types ostensibly become obsolete when programs can reveal themselves through glass frontages. This notion results in a homogenous expression for a diversity of architectural objects.

It is an ironic result, then, that so many contemporary buildings do not distinguish themselves in any manner apart from their scale. Many houses appear, in the words of Scott Cohen, as "miniature institutions." Lord Foster has no "house," for example. His residences in Japan (1992), and in Corsica (1993), as well as the Kwee home in Singapore (2009), all appear as public structures in homunculoid form. Given this, it is also interesting that his civic buildings don't look particularly civic. There is little that would distinguish his Supreme Court in Singapore from a mall.

This quintessentially modern notion—that anything may look like anything else—remains on the march. The Trojan Horse becomes the protagonist in

Frank Furness, Smoking Room, Furness House, Philadelphia, PA

an abstracted landscape, where the "finish fetish" of facades results in the free play of optical effect. The vulgarity of postmodern commercial architecture yields a complementary result. As one sees at South China Mall, or at Providence Place, a common solution for the exterior is a series of arbitrary expressions. This is less the Venturian duck than an *opéra bouffe* of genres. Yankee clock towers, faux-renovated factories, domes, and porticos appear. Anything can look like anything. The stylistic "inhabitation" of empty typologies appears to be merely a stratagem of last resort, a kind of taxidermy.[10] The great mass covers itself in fragments of dead architecture to conceal the fact that it is, in reality, post-architectural.

Against this backdrop, Jean Nouvel and Philippe Starck's 1986 proposal for the Tokyo Opera now seems brilliantly conclusive. In this project, the attempt to retain any correlation between massing and contents is cleverly, and cynically, resigned. Instead, the building is imagined as pure beauty-object, a pregnant black mass. The project reads not as willful perversity, but as the inevitable conclusion of a process begun with Garnier's Opéra, over a century earlier. The eternal ambiguity of interiors and their outward expressions, unresolved by Modernism, results in a kind of ironic muteness—the only choice when all remaining options are kitsch. The exterior can no longer be articulated, and must be passed over in silence.

Homunculism & Gigantism

We live in an era in which market forces push familiar objects toward extremes of dimension. All is elastic. Buildings, vehicles, meals and their packaging—and people, not least—are being "upsized." At the same time, the cultural imagination has been seized by miniaturized consumables, which grow ever smaller with microchips, semi-conductors, and integrated circuitry. Economies of scale exert an "Alice in Wonderland" effect on the physical world. These sometimes create value through "dumping," in which the consumer becomes a sink for huge capacities of cheap output. In the modern Karnaks of Costco and Home Depot, anything can be had in great amounts, for surprisingly little money. By contrast, expensive technical commodities arrive in increasingly small packages.

This recalls the nightmares of nuclear age pop culture, in which people and objects change size via the magic of the laboratory: films such as the *Attack of the 50 Foot Woman* (1958), *The Incredible Shrinking Man* (1957), and *Fantastic Voyage* (1966). Sci-fi Gullivars dramatize the relativizing experience of the contemporary subject who is continually finding him- or herself rescaled. Whether the inhabitant of a swollen body in a shrinking apartment, or a reduced consumer in a Brobdingnagian retail space, the unstable character of one's modern life involves—like Kant's sublime—a radical encounter with metrics.

Architecture and urbanism are not exempt from this. An inevitable result is the physical compression of buildings in tony areas. Designs retain their conventional appointments, while occupying ever smaller envelopes. Affordability leads, as we will see, to the replication of familiar compositions at miniature scales. The corollary is a dilation of real estate in marginal areas, in suburbs and remote locations, where malls and large houses can be made cheaply. This is the realm of the McMansion, which so often inflates the "classical" by means of plastics and stucco. The real estate bubble has its own pneumatic design language, which takes objects and blows them up.

In this process, an expanded scalar spectrum emerges. At the minor end is the *homunculus*. This includes any miniature that copies a normally-sized precedent. The homunculus does not substitute part for whole; rather, there is an attempt to replicate the original through reduction. In many European and African magical traditions, the familiar of the witch is imagined in this way, as a tiny person comprising the usual limbs and features. It is also true of gnomes and elves in Germany and Nordic countries. The

1. Miniature of the Met Life Building, New York City
2. "Herman," a German Giant rabbit, and his owner

1. Bernard Maybeck, Palace of Fine Arts, San Francisco
2. Set for *Aida*   3. Otto Kohtz, Reichshaus Project, Berlin

4. Iofan, Shchuko and Gelfreikh, Palace of the Soviets, Moscow
5. Hans Poelzig, Office and Exhibition Building for Hamburg

European version was said to be conjured from mandrake, a root with frequently humanoid form. Mandrake was rumored to take root from the morbid ejaculation of hanged men, and was thus harvested under trees used as gibbets.[1]

The homunculus plays on fears of the abnormal, and assumptions about the criminality of small people. In folk traditions, the little man is neither adult nor child, and is liminal with respect to categories of personhood. As a result he has commonly been considered untrustworthy, but also magical or lucky. The leprechaun is a good example. Recently, little people have played similar roles in the films of Terry Gilliam and David Lynch. Dr. Evil's sinister "Mini-Me" is now iconic, but examples are common—such as the 2006 comedy *Little Man*, in which a midget ex-con poses as a toddler. Their plight is that of many ambiguous social beings, as described by Marcel Mauss in his *General Theory of Magic*.[2] Similar assumptions exist regarding uncannily wizened children, such as the street urchin, the clairvoyant, or (in recent pop culture) the youthful vampire.[3]

As noted, the homunculoid building expresses economic forces exerted on scale. In this case, it is a downward pressure—the impetus for a building to shrink, while retaining the gross morphology of its type. Homunculism is most commonly a result of real estate as commercial product. It occurs, for example, when houses are shrunk to fit an "optimum" number on a site, as determined in the process of speculative development. Ever-smaller spaces are allocated to each unit. The shrinking Asian luxury apartment—and its burgeoning cost per square meter—is such a case. This is now a commonplace in most global cities, which are subject to similar influences.

The unnerving appearance of the typical homunculus is due, in part, to its lack of compromise with reduced size. The building is scaled down proportionally, as Solon Beman's grandstand was inflated. Only minor transformations of the object occur during reduction. In fact, tiny buildings often affect a kind of pomposity. This is the case in the mushrooming residential tracts of Ho Chi Minh City, where narrow homes are built with priapic temple-fronts and Rococo flourishes. A similar confusion occurs in Shanghainese "villa" subdivisions, where high market prices incentivize the developer to reduce each to the minimum. "Value" is communicated not through size, but through ostentatious treatments. The resulting cottages are often expressed as large homes. This fits neatly into Shanghainese traditions, where a simple house was often entered by means of a monumental gate; there was, and is, no belief that expression and size need be proportionate.[4]

Some architects, however, have harnessed this effect to create a new language of building, positing very complex buildings at very small sizes. This is the radical scalar effect of the Japanese "dog house," in the works of Atelier Bow Wow, SANAA, and others. These are often less than 100 square meters in reality. In the hands of sophisticated architects, such miniaturization becomes a mode of exploration in the reorganization of the house, much to the benefit of the design. House Tower (2006), by Bow Wow is one such work, and their Gae House (2003) and Tread Machiya House (2008) play a similar game with a richness of results.

The homunculus exists somewhere between building and model; that is, between the object and its representation. The eye refuses to grant it a status due to

1. Window on the World Amusement Park, Shenzhen, PRC
2. George Grosz, *The Writer Max-Hermann Neisse*, 1925

3. Max Berg, Jarhunderthalle, Breslau   4. Ronchamp at 60% of full scale, Zhengzhou, PRC   5. Lev Rudnev, Moscow State University

architectural works. It remains an incomplete individual, despite having a full complement of parts. This effect is particularly keen when the building can be read against its surroundings, against conventions of type, or against precedents. One sees this, for example, in the village of Zhengzhou, in China's Henan Province, where a reduced version of Le Corbusier's chapel at Ronchamp has been constructed. In this case, the surrounding topiaries reveal the lie, in much the same manner as the crowd in Beman's giant. This Ronchamp is 60% of actual size, and is used as a house. The same happens in those cityscapes that are shrunk for our entertainment, such as the New York and Venice of Las Vegas. A disproportion occurs, and the anamorphic illusion is often compromised from certain viewpoints, especially when seen against adjacent buildings. The Window on the World and Splendid China theme parks in Shenzhen create similar disjunctions, such as placing the US Capitol near Mount Rushmore. Both stand next to a small tree that appears enormous in comparison. Such miniaturization given rise to a range of Asian tourist attractions and amusement areas, such as Singapore's brilliantly named Lilliputt golf course.

It is also worth remarking that shrinkage can occur in one or two dimensions, leaving the third unaffected. This is a very suggestive frontier at which homunculism meets distortion—a sort of gray area between the two. Examples include the apartment typologies developed on small plots in Hong Kong, during the property boom of the 1980s and 1990s. These are amazing, because their footprint and plan have been down-scaled, while their height has been increased. The result is an exaggerated pin-tower, which appears to have been stretched in one axis.[5]

At the other end of the scalar spectrum is *gigantism*. The giant is likewise one of the central forms in the historical imaginary of horror and monstrosity. As with the homunculus, his deviance has to do with size. Variations include the ogre, Goliath, King Kong, and Gargantua, and extend to mythologies even older than Gog and Magog in the Hebrew bible. Many figures of Greek mythology were thought to be enormous—such as Theseus and Ajax—and a distinct race of giants were described in ongoing conflict with the gods of Olympus.

The gigantic building is not the same as the blob or the megastructure. The latter are notable for their extensiveness, polymorphism and complexity. Gigantism is far simpler. It occurs when something is enlarged proportionally. Gigantism is not merely largesse; it is the property of something being *bigger than it should*, being inappropriate to tradition. That is to say, it is a matter of scale, and not size. The result is frightening, but also sublime. Such titans have, in the words of Melville, an "appalling beauty."[6] Their greatness, relative to our expectations, produces an emotive resonance.

As we mention above, gigantism has much to do with a typological instability inherent in modernity. Certainly, it reflects the expansion of commercial spaces. But it also emphasizes the increasingly problematic status of public building in an urban context. As the city undergoes enlargement—as houses become mansions, shops become department stores, and low-rises become high-rises—civic works must expand to retain a proportional importance. This has produced a crisis of expectations, which can be read in the hyperbolic one-upmanship of *fin-de-siecle* architectures. Take, for example, Fernand Janin's City

1

2

3

4

Hall study, which formed part of Burnham and Bennett's famous 1909 Plan of Chicago. The architect's rendering shows St. Peters re-imagined as a skyscraper: a huge ballistic projection, each tier a giant in itself. The building blocks of Janin's colossus are other grand edifices, which are stacked like tiny quotations. His front entrance is the Pantheon; on its roof, the Parthenon; to either side stands a Baroque pinnacle after the manner of Borromini's St. Ivo. Behind this pile are rendered the great commercial volumes of Michigan Avenue, homunculized by comparison.

Such hyperbole may not seem so odd in context. In fact, the upsizing of conventions was common at this time, and at what must have seemed like exponential leaps in scale and complexity. Throughout the Loop, new blocks were shattering the expected limits of construction. Edifices such as the Congress Hotel (1908) must have seemed enormous, especially to those accustomed to 19th-century precedents. Holabird and Roche's 1917-18 study for North Michigan Avenue seems a caricature of White City Chicago, with each inflated classical object more monumental than the next. The Merchandise Mart, built nearby in 1930, was so vast as to remain, for some time, the largest concentration of floor space in the world; it required the Pentagon to surpass it. Even Janin's *outré* vision was rivalled by Frank Lloyd Wright's project for the National Life Insurance building, 15 years later. Wright's proposal echoed the new tower vocabularies explored by New Yorkers such as Raymond Hood and Hugh Ferris, uplit Art Deco ziggurats of Olympian aspect.

Gigantism is here associated with the identity— what would now be called the "branding"—of the commercial and civic building. It is not surprising, then,

1. Johann Fischer von Erlach, Temple of Zeus   2. Fernand Janin, study for Chicago City Hall   3. Wilhelm Kreis, Totenburgen   4. Étienne Louis Boulée, large church (project)

that a similar scalar brinkmanship was being assayed for ideological projects in other contexts. This was certainly the case with French symbolic works, described elsewhere in this book. Boullée's Palais de Justice (1780s) Metropolitan Church (1781-1782), and Palais National (1792) were immense, taking a radically clarified Neoclassicism to Alpine scale. These were later echoed in Albert Speer's colossal proposal for Berlin's Volkshalle, and also in Wilhelm Kreis' *Totenburgen* (castles of the dead), Nazi war memorials to be built at former battlefields.[7] The Soviets were equally ambitious. Boris M. Iofan's 1934 perspective for the Palace of the Soviets shows a style not unlike Janin's (with a giant Lenin perched on top). Alternative versions by Armando Brazini[8] preserve the vastness. In each case, microbial humans litter the foreground. Konstantin Melnikov's 1934 project for the Ministry of Heavy Industry shows the sublime plasticity of constructivist geometries; the massing appears to stack impossible buildings on top of each other. These were not merely speculations. The main building of Moscow State University (1949-53), by Lev Vladimirovich Rudnev, looks similarly far-fetched. It remains the tallest educational building in the world. Rome's famously lamented Monument to Vittorio Emanuelle II (1911-35), by Giuseppe Sacconi, takes advantage of the Capitoline Hill to project a picturesque height, and terracing that intentionally appears to reduce the visitor to negligibility.

Such works—whether viewed in the flesh or in photograph—have much to do with the three dimensionality of the object. These are powerfully, incontrovertibly *positive*. There are negative analogues, however, which are no less devastating in their emotive force. Clearly, the master of the gigantic interior remains

Piranesi, and the *veduta* of the Carceri still produce a visceral response. The sublimity is like vertigo; it is extraordinary to imagine a space that appears architectural, yet would be nearly impossible to traverse. The interiors of the Carceri are great subterranean gorges, suggesting Tolkein landscapes or the passes of China's Huangshan, edged by tiny boardwalks. The latter are like additive elements, compromises made to allow for human occupation. A person cannot properly inhabit the space; we can merely beetle about the edges. This is the disconcerting effect of the opening scene of Ridley Scott's *Alien* (1979), in which the derelict starship of a giant race is discovered by the crew of Nostromo. As the corpse of the extraterrestrial is approached, the explorers must negotiate stairs that are half their own height. The interior of Boullée's Metropolitan Church produces a similar vision. It is a sense of enormity actually achieved in some built works, such as Max Berg's Jahrhunderthalle for the 1913 Breslau Exhibition and Tony Garnier's abattoir at La Mouche in Lyons, constructed in 1917. Today, it can be felt in the heroic atria of works such as the 2005 New South China Mall—known as the "Great Mall of China"—in Dongguan, and in Helmut Jahn's own *Speerlicher* James R. Thompson Center (1985) in Chicago.

It is interesting that, in many of the previous images and buildings (whether giants or homunculi) the presence of the human figure is required to demonstrate the deviant scaling of the object. This is due precisely to the peculiarity of the trope, which sets the giant building apart from, for example, the expo center or mega-mall. The resizing happens, as we point out, proportionally. In some cases, such as Janin's City Hall proposal, the new vastness is seized as an opportunity to innovate: by piling famous

archetypes atop and beside one another, for example. Often, however, there are few changes. The ability to ignore the consequences of scale has, moreover, only been exacerbated by the abstraction of modern vocabularies. This is the case, for example, with the Miesian building—if not with Mies' own—where magnification and reduction can occur without being immediately apparent. This is the secret behind projects such as SANAA's Small House (1999) and S-House (1997), which can only be measured by looking at doors, or at objects in the surrounding context. These buildings make no attempt to be deceptive. They simply originate in a language of lightness and extrusion that has little inherent dimensionality.

This is even more the case in the contemporary moment, in which a single anti-scalar element—the pattern—provides a major organizing element in many design strategies. Size, like value, has become an elusive quantum, subject to obfuscation. In a very real sense, the deviant character of large buildings no longer exists. At least, these can not be so easily recognized, and have lost their old power to scandalize.

ARC Studio / RSP, The Pinnacle@Duxton, Singapore, photographed by Darren Soh

Solidity, mass, stereotomy

Solidity is a truly horrid thing; an irreconcilable, existential terror. The solid object provides no space, either physically or philosophically, for inhabitation. Here again, nature plays the role of our antithesis—but it does so not, as before, through aggressive growth. Rather, it discomfits by means of impenetrability, its "thingly" resistance to social appropriation. The rock is mute, indelible, the other of consciousness and social life.

Our mythologies tell of constant traffic between flesh and earth. Adam was forged from "mortal clay" in an act of god, awesome and violent. The Golem, Frankenstein's Judaic antecedent, was also made of mud. Its name connotes formlessness, a lack of organic articulation—a "lump," animated by the spirit of words. The Greeks imagined the Amazons to have likewise been galvanized from earth. Pandora was sculpted to bewitch men, as revenge for the theft of fire by Prometheus (who had also created humans from clay). Other creation myths are nearly identical: the Enuma Elish; the Egyptian tale of Khnum; Nuwa, in Chinese legend, and African and South American versions.

The reverse transformation, of flesh into stone, is a no less worrying idea. It is not by accident that witnesses to horrors are described as "petrified." Medusa ossified all who looked upon her, most famously when her head

was brandished at Atlas and Phineus. Apollo and Artemis turned Niobe to stone. The Basilisk did the same, as did witches in more recent European folklore. Dutch folk tales included goblins that would become statuary if touched by sunlight, as would trolls in Nordic tradition. Stone giants and warriors appear in both Western and Asian folklores.

Petrification was also a trope of architectural origins. Vitruvius attributed the Erectheion Caryatids to the women of a Peloponnesian town, turned to stone for betraying Athens. Celtic Christians told a similar story about the Merry Maidens in Cornwall, and other dolmens associated with pagan revelry: girls were punished for dancing on a Sunday. As such, their fate parallels a more realist theory of classical ornament, in which the vocabulary of early wood joinery was "frozen" in stone.

In other versions, rock represents an unmediated or crude basis of dwelling. Caverns and mountain hollows have long been cast as the home of the non-human: dwarves, dragons, trolls, and their ilk. At the least, such occupation connotes primeval, or pre-cultural, origins. We still evoke the "caveman" as the foil of the modern person, as he who has not yet asserted mastery over the environment. Images of cave dwelling still have the power to shock, as in the burrow-houses of Shanxi, or the village of Zhongdong in Guizhou Province, in China—in the latter, the standard rural hamlet sits below the vault, and the sky itself appears to have been replaced by the underbelly of the hillside.

The proximity of this *unheimlich* solidity characterizes the Andalusian town of Setenil De Las Bodegas, where dwellings shelter below a natural projection of rock. The undercroft appears like a nacreous cloud, hovering over the streets of Setenil, opalescent and bulging. The roofs and walls of the buildings occasionally dip to accommodate its prominence. Even the street corridor—that which is supposed to provide an access for light—looks sat upon.

This contrast is nauseating. It represents the very other of the *heimlich*: the postcard village over-girded by such solidity, by an unbearable evacuation of life. The rock speaks of mineral patience, the grinding geological timescale that reduces human experience to negligibility. This quality of the Setenil massif was recognized elsewhere by Bernini, who used stone precisely for its power "to make of time a thing stupendous."[1] The lively sculpture, like the looming overhang or counterscarp, embodies Kant's sublime: that moment in which the cosmic is brought into comparison with the metrics of our finitude. The

1. Zhongdong Village, Guizhou Province, PRC   2. Town of Stenil De Las Bodegas, Andalusia, Spain   3. Sleeper House, St Louis, MI

1

2

3

1, 2. Hang Na Villa, Dalat, Vietnam   3. Jerome, Cappadocia

4

5

6

4. Filip Dujardin, from *Fictions,* 2010   5. Frank Furness, Manufacturer's National Bank, Philadelphia   6. false windows at party wall, London

protuberance of Setenil is the Sword of Damocles as blunt object. The Spanish cottages contain familiar components: walls, doors, windows, and the like. By contrast, there is the ontic irreducibility of stone. It presents itself as brute co-extensiveness, where the physical becomes metaphysical.

A similar effect occurs in the Chapel of St. Gildas, Brittany, where the ecclesiastical object huddles beneath an outcrop of granite. The chapel conceals a cave, where Gildas is said to have evangelized among the local pagans. In many respects, it appears intersected with the hillside; shafts of rock make contact both above and below, and the natural face of the bluff juts abruptly into the prayer hall. There appears a continual exchange between the pointed curvatures of boulders, and the geometries of a country Gothic vocabulary. In an odd moment, the church bell is attached directly to the granite face, in lieu of a steeple. St. Gildas is a compelling balance of the constructed and the excavated. The hill town of Kandovan, in Iran, presents a similar interpelation, in which simple sheds extend the hollow stone chimneys to the exterior.

A more rhetorical version appears in French didactic projects, Romantic gardens and *architectures parlantes*. The gardens at Ermenonville included an allegorical landscape of hermit caves, popular in the late 18th century and thereafter, carved into hillsides. Likewise Claude-Louis Chatelet's Le Rocher at Folie Saint-James (1777-80), in which a Doric nymphaeum stands excavated from rock with "rude simplicity." The composition was later borrowed by Le Corbusier in a scheme for the Villa Meyer.[2] An exploration of this same theme was the Fete de la Federation by Étienne-Louis Boullée (1790), a scenographic folly that merges the iconic temple-

1. Lycian tombs, Fethiye, Turkey   2. Tomb of Midas, Afyon, Turkey
3. St. Gildas Chapel, Brittany, France   4. Acoustic mirror, Yorkshire, UK

front with a miniaturized crag reminiscent of those at Hausmann's Parc des Buttes-Chaumont.[3] Most radical among these is Boullée's cenotaph for Isaac Newton (1784). The arch-symbolist's insertion of a dark natural defile, a sort of geomorphic vagina, into the floor of his memorial contrasts in scale and character with the curved colonnade that wraps its perimeter. Under an abstracted firmament, the delicate orders of this proscenium appear as the very abstraction of human achievements. The mirroring of the rude and the Hellenic, nature and artifice, occurs again when the proscenium of columns is mimicked on the exterior by a ring of trees.

Such cases are striking, perhaps, as they present a condition in which highly conventional architecture abuts the purely geophysical. In other examples, however, these two are completely superimposed. Cities and temples have been carved from mountains, either superficially or in a profundity of caves and burrows. These environments, carved or extracted, are more properly stereotomic.

This atmosphere is powerfully communicated in architectures chiseled from the surfaces of great massifs. The Treasury at Petra, Jordan, demonstrates an extraordinary contrast between a delicacy of ornamental vocabulary and the brutality of the stone mountain. A similar effect

Étienne-Louis Boullée, Cenotaph for Isaac Newton

is produced by numerous examples of Turkish and Indian temple architecture, such as the Tombs of Caria in Kaunos (4th century B.C.), and the Phrygian Tomb of Midas (8th century).[4] These are suggestive, in part, because their failure to domesticate the mountain is so obvious. As tombs and temples, this inability becomes part of their metaphysical program. This is effective in the Tomb of Amyntas in Fethiye (4th century B.C.), where a rather crude rectilinear extraction frames the more lissome and decorative façades within. Perhaps most evocative is the manner in which the stratigraphic structure of the stone continues to express itself, resisting assimilation into artifice. This is seen in the striated patterning, for example, which passes through the hill and building alike, irrespective of form, massing, or volume. The "natural" and incised areas appear at times continuous and at others contrasted, as in the many grottoes found at Maijishan in East Gansu province, China. In some of these, the color and texture of the stone provide a unity; elsewhere, the extreme rustication or clay surface of the mountain make the Buddhist structures appear inserted. The same is true of the many loess cave dwellings that are an historical typology of this region. This is urbanism as speleology, suggesting alien modes of tubular organization.

The hewn churches of Lalibela (c.13th century) are a vertical permutation, being carved not into a hillside but instead from bedrock beneath the soil of Northern Ethiopia. Each stands in its own trench, having been excavated downwards. As such, there is great ambiguity, here, between solid and void, figure and ground. The churches fill their pits like objects. The lack of overt veining or patterning in the stone delays the realization that these monolithic buildings would otherwise be extensions of the

surrounding rock faces. That is, the church that appears so
"positive" and object-like is in fact a negativity imposed
upon continuous matter.

There is a lingering aura of myth and ancient
history about these examples, but one also notes a similar
interest among early Modernists in exploring the aesthetics
of the solid. The Expressionists in particular produced many
buildings, the moulded curvilinearity of which appeared to
be worked from a clay-like plasticity. The House of the
Grand Duke Ernst Ludwig (1899-1901) in Darmstadt's
artists' colony, by Joseph Maria Olbrich, is typical of this
effect. Here, the massing and ornament appear to merge
with a collection of sculptural works in a single contiguity,
a "goop" that unites all. A complementarity of white stone
and stucco establishes the effect. Drawings for Henri van
de Velde's Werkbund theatre project for Cologne (1914)
show a similar intention, a gooeyness reminiscent of Eric
Mendelsohn. A similar degree of the monolithic was
achieved, through a different technique, by Charles Rennie
Mackintosh, in his Glasgow Art School (1896-1909). Here,
taut masonry—a stereotomy of stacked blocks—does the
work, as it did in highly perverse works by Frank Furness,
including the National Bank of the Republic (1883) and
the alarming Provident Life and Trust Building (1878-9),
both in Philadelphia.

This line of exploration perhaps found its apex
in the works of Hans Poelzig. Poelzig was, as much as
any of his contemporaries, the architect of the solid. This
may be due to the fact that his buildings where designed
stereotomically; the models for most were directly
excavated from clay. A maquette of his proposed Bismarck
Memorial, Second Scheme (1911) shows this. There is

1. Luigi Moretti, project for the Church of the Concilio Sancta Maria
Mater Ecclesiae, Rome   2. Moretti, parking garage at Villa Borghese,
Rome   3. Hans Poelzig, Chemical Factory, Luban, Poland

1

2

3

little consideration of tectonics, here; the project is clearly conceived as continuous matter. The result is almost revoltingly plastic, as was his project for a Fire Station in Dresden (1969-7). The architect's factory buildings for Luban (1911) and Breslau (1906-8), and his water tower for Hamburg (ca. 1910) were likewise driven by an expression of massiveness.

The infrastructural character of these large production facilities was not obscured behind a mask of humanism. Instead, the depth of the wall is celebrated outright. But solidity was even more striking at the Großes Schauspielhaus (1919), in which Poelzig developed his language of the cavernous. Both the famous entry vestibule and main theatre appear excavated from a palpable thickness. In the grand hall, rings of dripping pendentives suggest eons of calcification. These organize themselves into hive-like formations, which fall toward the floor as stalactites. This was a feat of artifice, as there was, in fact, nothing much solid about the building at all. The art critic Karl Scheffler noted, with regret, that this "colossal" and "solid-looking" object was a "sham," constructed like a Hollywood set from plasterboard.[5] It might not be surprising, given this, to know that Poelzig produced a fanciful reconstruction of the Prague Ghetto for Carl Boesse and Paul Weneger's 1920 film *Der Golem*. In Poelzig's dreamlike version, the urbanism of the Jewish quarter is absolutely Golem-like: earthen and lumpen, with fragments of architecture, timber beams and crepuscular windows, adrift within its mucky facades.

There is here a kind of irrationalist impulse— or rather, an ambivalent approach to rationalism of the kind exploited by Hitler—which seems to find itself in

1. Poelzig, Grosses Schauspeilhaus, Berlin   2. coastal bunker, California   3. Andre Bloc, Structure Habitacle II

an aesthetics of the massive. It is an ersatz primitivism, a return to "thingliness" which may be aesthetically linked to mysticism, and to the folklore of the Grimms and the Golem. Such a current is strongly felt among the Expressionists, the modernity of whom appears to have been disguised behind an obfuscation of emotion and spiritualism, in the way that the Deutscher Werkbund invoked John Ruskin's notion of "craft."[6]

This impulse endures, even within the mature Modernist program. The mass remains a powerful presence, occasionally coming back into fashion: with the later works of Le Corbusier, with Paul Rudolph, Brutalism, and Asian Metabolism. It appears, certainly, in iconoclastic works, where a certain mysticism remains. These include projects like Gottfried Bohm's Pilgrimage Church in Neviges (1963-72), which combines the monolithic with a medieval revivalism. Or Friedrich Kiesler's Endless House (1950), a concrete egg intended to produce a pure spatial continuum. Experiments such as the Pavillon de Plâtre (1965) and Habitacle II (1964) by André Bloc, re-presented familiar forms within a robustly sculptural language. Luigi Moretti was likewise a champion of the monolithic, in his Church of the Concilio Sancta Maria Mater Ecclesiae (1965-70), the Villa La Saracena (1953-7), and the Underground Parking Garage at the Villa Borghese (1965-72), which is perhaps the most effective expression of the cavernous since Poelzig. We see a similar anti-planar fixation in Spanish organicism of the kind championed in the Mercado de Daimiel (1955) and building for the Dólar publishing house (1974) by Miguel Fisac; and in Francisco Sáenz de Oisa's Santuario de Arantzazu (1950-4). Likewise, one finds solidity persisting as a signifier of radical

experiment, as in the 1970s "fonction oblique" projects of Jean Nouvel and Paul Virilio. At the same time, this work is reminiscent of infrastructures and buildings where solidity was a matter of technical requirement, such as the Atlantic Coast bunkers documented by Virilio himself.

However, little experimentation remains in the field of solidity. Lightness would appear to better suit the productive logic of industrial capital—monolithic construction, its weight and excess, is fundamentally out of step with the laminations of the contemporary constructive mentality. Solidity appears iconoclastic and reactionary, associated perhaps more with the thick poche of pre-modernism. It has everything to with the real: that is, the encounter with an un-abstract and intractable physicality. Nothing could appear less accommodating, particularly in the era of the virtual.

Sets for the film *Der Golem*, designed by Hans Poelzig

Distortion: Deformity and Disproportion

We turn, finally, to two types of distortion. The first is *deformity*, in which the morphology of an object, or piece thereof, is contrary to expectation. The result appears "misshapen" or "disfigured." The second is *disproportion*, in which one corporate element is out of scale in comparison to others.

Distortion is always read against a norm, as ugliness is defined against beauty. Horror of the dysmorphic invokes the classical notion that certain formal conventions are somehow *correct*—at least, they are in keeping with the aesthetic principles of nature itself. Such was the assumption of Platonic idealism. More to our purposes, it was the belief of Vitruvius, who posited that architectural composition should relate to the biometrics of the human head, torso, and limbs. Of course, this is a purely analogical argument. Such prejudices are merely customary—that is, they are "positive" and not naturally given. This is clearly the case, for example, when one considers the global variety of beautifications considered strange to a Western eye: bound feet, the ringed necks of the Burmese Padaung and South African Ndebele, or the lip and ear plates of the Kayapo, Makonde, and Mursi. But the naturalization of the beauty ideal dies hard, perhaps because we are reluctant to accept the notion that something so acutely felt might also be utterly arbitrary.

By definition, distortion is framed by recognizable normality. This is beautifully illustrated in *La Cena*, a painting by Antonio López Garcia. Here, the localized deformity of the adult head, at right, occurs within a primarily realist mode of representation. The face of the child can be read as a benchmark, a grounding of the language of the piece. The horrible visage of the mother introduces a world of meaningful instability. Is this a shift into a language of abstraction? Does this figure inhabit the same space and time as the child? Similar questions emerge in the "dreadful" images of Francis Bacon, where moments of precise depiction sharpen the indistinct terror of the surrounding deformities.[1] In his "Study After Velasquez's Portrait of Pope Innocent X," for example, the mouth plays this role, as does the right eye in his 1971 "Self-Portrait."

Antonio López Garcia, *La Cena*, 1971-80

1. MVRDV, VPRO Headquarters, Hilversum   2. Crooked House, Sopot, Poland   3. Church spire, Chesterfield, UK   4. Frank Gehry, Lews Building, Cleveland, OH   5. Collapsed farmouse, USA

6 7

In a loose sense, many of the architectural horrors we have discussed so far are "de-formed." All are, to a degree, deviant with respect to formal conventions. However, there remains the problem of "simple" deformity: that is, when whole or part are atypical compared to a generally "normal" body. This is quite distinct from the exquisite corpse, for example, which breaks no internal rule—rather, it is aberrant for comprising only exceptions.

Likewise, one can violate conventions without appearing deformed. As we discuss elsewhere, clones and twins have often been thought to offend the natural order of personhood. There is, however, nothing anatomically awry. In much the same way, a midget is usually defined as a proportionally correct person, albeit down-scaled. They are disproportionate with respect to the average, but not within themselves. These are what we might call "para-deformities," the deviance of which is apprehended through broader social meanings.

By contrast, we react viscerally to that which appears overtly dysmorphic. This is far less arbitrary in the case of human and animal bodies. Such a reaction is provoked, for example, by the "Elephant Man" Joseph Merrick—in the apparent excess of his skin with respect to

6. Francis Bacon, *Self-Portrait*, 1971 7. shock, by Tex Avery

his body. Merrick's presumed neurofibromatosis produced both distortions and disproportions: in the composition of face, head and torso, and in the scale, position, and shape of features. The nature of Merrick's body appears clearly "incorrect" with respect to the normative efficiency of the bodily surface. Human skin is expected to sit quite closely upon the musculature, as if taut. Of course, Merrick is not "unnatural;" his body is simply a permutation of the human genome. But it is safe to say that our reaction of fascination and horror has very much to do with the sense that he is somehow a perversion of God's order.

Distortions in architecture happen under many different circumstances. A romantic variant are those that occur through the process of weathering, as in an abandoned or ruined timber building. Sagging and fatigue are inherent effects of decomposition, and tend to alter the geometry of the structure in a uniform manner, giving the impression it has been warped, in part or whole. Structurally interdependent members often fail beautifully together, as the logic of their construction translates into the coherence of their decomposition. There is a consistency to the resulting geometry—the degree and distance of sagging, as well as the form of curvatures—through which the original structure can be inferred. This is supported by our memory of vernacular types, which allow one to guess how such objects would have originally appeared. We do this, for example, when viewing the famous bent spire of Chesterfield, England, which fell victim to the contraction of timber beams. It appears today like a sinister (or perhaps amusing) corkscrew; at the same time, the original can be clearly imagined. This principle is at work, also, in "fisheye" photographs. Here, our eye presumes the rules

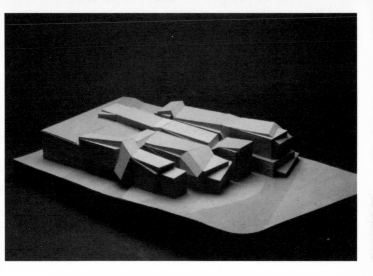

of perspective themselves: the apparent "bending" of space registers against our internal knowledge of the standard 35mm image.

Likewise, distortions emerge when formal conventions are pressured by constraints of site or program. This may result in an innovation that is considered beautiful, or in a compromise that seems ugly or laughable. Take, for example, an inevitable product of urban real estate, the awkward but valuable site. These often result from cadastral accidents: tiny wedges and slivers, crooked and bent residuals, or plots that are absurdly long with respect to their frontage. These frequently stand at locations too attractive to remain undeveloped, and curious structures emerge.

London's so-called "Thin House" in Thurloe Square, which appears to winnow to an edge, is the result of such a case. The site is an inhospitable triangle, with one acute corner. The Thin House adapts to it in a very matter-of-fact way, spreading itself almost to the limits of the available footprint. The Georgian vocabulary establishes

Eisenman Architects, Emory Center for the Arts, Atlanta

1. Lucy McRae, Germination Day One, 2008   2. "Mr. Creosote,"
Monty Python's Meaning of Life, 1983   3. Deformation of a bus, after
Richard Scarry   4. "Thin House," Thurloe Square, London, UK

its scale, and makes the diminution appear unusually powerful. It is a composition that has been distorted in one dimension, in depth. What is striking about Thin House, apart from its Dickensian name, is that the building appears to compromise only little with its strange predicament. It remains purely frontal, addressing the street and ignoring the corner. A similar, although far less handsome example exists at Sixth Avenue in Singapore. Here, the developer's palazzo is shoehorned into another triangular site. It is yet further constrained by urban design guidelines, which mandate that the resulting wedge be augmented by two pitched roofs. The treatment of the house as an antique confection does not match the plasticity of the envelope. In clinging to a faux-Paladian frontality, the resulting volume appears compressed. The decision to express one side of the triangle as a front (and the other as rear) has produced a profoundly misshapen object.

A similar quandary has given rise to very different products: for example, the Flatiron Building in New York, as well as a famous art deco block at the acute intersection of Wukang and Huaihai roads, in Shanghai. Here, the arrowhead geometry of the parcels molded the Neoclassical vocabulary into striking ornamented prows. These were more satisfying resolutions, as their architects acknowledged the importance of the corner, and abandoned frontality as a compositional technique; instead, the corner was transformed into a kind of micro-facade familiar from European urban buildings.[2]

In other cases, deformity is intentional and playful, part of a self-conscious design strategy. It becomes rhetorical, as a method of adding character. This is the case with the Crooked House (2003), a shopping center in

Sopot, Poland. The principal facade has been subjected to a curvilinear transformation that makes it appear to "sway" laterally, as well as to bulge and recede as if buckling. This is reminiscent of a hall of mirrors, or a fun house in which curved surfaces create a novelty environment. In this case, the precise geometry of the deformation appears unimportant to the design; it is simply an effect.

There is a clear difference between distortion used as a totalizing strategy, and instances wherein it is employed locally. In the former, deformation has a stylistic aspect. This may be true even in buildings where the deformity is used to produce new spatial conditions, as at MVRDV's VPRO. Certainly, the architects' extensive use of the ramped plate does give rise to innovations, such as the relegation of staircases to a supporting role in vertical circulation. It likewise results in a range of unusual geometrical intersections between surfaces. More than anything, the bulging of the floor alters the normal proportion of circulation to program, an exchange of curved and ramped slabs for flat ones (as in certain parking garages). This gives the interior an improvisational, meandering feel.[3]

VPRO embodies an approach in which distortion appears everywhere; the building becomes a performance of willful variability. Deformity is rather differently handled in the work of Peter Eisenman. As we have noted with respect to cloning, works such as Rebstock and Emory Center for the Arts continue the architect's emphasis on the legibility of particular formal operations, on the building as the record of a design process. This is achieved through differential distortion, applied to a typological series—of generic bars, say, or cubic volumes. These may be read against one another, or against their implied prismatic origins. One can see the effect of Eisenman's operations on normative architectural elements: massing, volume, circulation, and the position and form of rooms in plan and section. In this sense, deformation is not simply a "shaping" of the envelope, as much as a method for re-ordering the substance of architecture.

For Preston Scott Cohen, as for Eisenman, the legibility of the distortion is urgent. Transformations of the architectural object—in part or whole—is a process that must be understood. In Cohen's work, the progressive metamorphosis is achieved through what might be called a "trouble-maker:" a sequence of projections, or the action of a rogue element. These enact a complex tug-of-war between idiosyncrasy and system, willfulness and determination. In the Torus House, for example, the unsettling device is a spline that meanders through the surfaces of the home, in such a way as to meaningfully alter the geometry of each. This method is opposed to MVRDV's, in which the deformity is a generalized effect that only ceases when the floor plates are cut by the planes of the building's envelope. It likewise differs from Eisenman's method, in which a series is shown in progressive states of change. Cohen's is a sort of surgical distortion, in which the spline, like a keloid, can be read in localized disturbances of its surroundings. The vortical effect of the line forces novel iterations of conventional elements, such as the light well, the stairwell, the *impluvium*, and so forth; the effect of three-dimensional curvature is to deny assumed relationships among orthogonal surfaces. The interloper obliges everything to change; Cohen then plays the game of partially normalizing these adaptations. The disturbance forces, in each case, a resolution. These predicaments are extraneous, and imposed. But they are also not gratuitous, as their logical consequences result in the production of surprising form.

All of these strategies rely on legibility, which in turn lends meaningful structure to deformation. That is to say: both the operations and their results may be comprehended. Anamorphosis is a similar technique—one that is organized around the production of a vista. The anamorphic projection, while it causes an object or space to appear misshapen from most everywhere, is resolved to normal appearance from a privileged viewpoint. This occurs in Renaissance pallazi, in shopping centers, and on sitcom sound-stages, where the perspective creates a sort of extreme hierarchy: the creation of one, perhaps two places from which the effect works. The goal is often to aggrandize a given composition, or to extend a stair or corridor into space that does not exist. The Scala Regia at the Vatican (1666), by Bernini, is a celebrated case. The diminution of the space in plan and section, and in the resulting distortion of the coffered ceiling, dramatically attenuates its appearance. Another fascinating example was produced by the architect of the Palace of Charles V, where an apparently "deep" stair is lodged within the depth of a single wall.

Finally, we would compare the deviant potential of deformity with that of disproportion. The latter is a fairly common aspect of everyday aesthetics. It is a technique used in cartoon and caricature, for example. Sometimes the enlargement of a single feature is used to produce ugliness, or to suggest a disproportion within the subject's personality. Elsewhere, it is employed to create "cute" distortions. For example, the women represented in Japanese *manga* and *anime* have eyes and breasts that are dramatically enlarged with respect to the rest of their anatomy. The former produces an infantile appearance, which combines fetishistically with an exaggerated fertility. The Bambi-like proportion of eye to face is in fact reminiscent of certain types of "charismatic megafauna:" baby seals, puppies, and the like.

Where architecture is concerned, it also seems true that human societies are more offended by deviations in shape than size. We have argued—with respect to gigantism, above—that the march of abstraction in modernism has led to a diminished sensitivity to scale. This is evident in buildings that rely on grids and patterns, but it is also a mainstay of bad classicism. The ornamental vocabulary of the typical McMansion, for example, depends much on the engorgement of features: pediments, cornices, columns, etcetera. This is due, in part, to misunderstanding of, or disregard for, the proportional conventions of classicism. But disproportion is also used to aggrandize and adapt. The priapic temple-front is, in Texas or Singapore, used to cool a four-car porch. The giant doorway helps to resolve the volumetric expression of a double-height entry gallery. Mis-sized wings hold "great rooms" and other recent contrivances.

In a less vulgar way, this was also a technique of Mannerist architects, who tested the tolerances of the antique vocabulary, and enthusiastically distanced themselves from ideals of naturalism. Scale was an effective way to emphasize artifice, and to highlight the arbitrary rules of the treatises. This is the case, for example, in Michelangelo's stair at the Laurentian Library, (c. 1571) which is so disproportionately scaled to the entry vestibule that surrounds it. The stair has an inappropriate largesse that inverts the expected relationship of a building and its contents. It is overbearing, and the room feels difficult to inhabit. A strange kind of hyper-plasticity dominates, as well as a diagonality in which the floor appears to subside. This almost obscene three-dimensionality is also present in the home of Giorgio Vasari at Arezzo (1542-50), in which the over-scaling of fireplace and coffers within a small room leads to an odd homogeneity—all the decorative elements in the room become more or less the same size. All are too big for their container, leading to a kind of comical pretentiousness. As with so many Mannerist stylings, disproportion was taken up in an even more exaggerated manner by the Postmodernists. This is clearly the technique of the gigantic keystone, à la Michael Graves, or Stanley Tigerman's great pediments of siding. More recently, this technique can be seen in the miniature house used by FAT to accomplish a radical scalar shift at their "Nonument" in the Hague (2006).

However, this technique appears somehow more articulate when it is not employed in the service of a device, or a stylistic identifier. For example, scale may be used to register a particular condition in the production of a building, a peculiarity of context or circumstance. All of this takes place in the roof of the Gae House (2003) by Atelier Bow Wow, which uses disproportion to a very skillful and efficient effect. Here, the homonculization of the Japanese "dog house"—the home that is proportionally down-scaled—is addressed by the normally sized roof. In proportional terms, this element is goofily large, overhanging at the eaves like a great hat. In fact, its size narrates the relative shrinking of the house, a fact of the

1. Home of Giorgio Vasari, Florence 2. Typical McMansion 3. Eiermann Memorial Church, Berlin 4. Michelangelo, Laurentian Library, Florence

urban economy within which it has been produced. The move is rhetorical, but not simply so: its giant quality is an index against which the scalar downshifting of the Japanese building can be read.

In a nearly opposite condition, the strange overhangs of Herzog and de Meuron's Ricola Europe factory and storage block (1993) work to domesticate the nearly scaleless mass of an industrial shed. The projections on either side are functional, as roofing that shelters the loading of trailers. However, their pellucid materiality—the silk-screen of the company logo on polycarbonate panels—makes it clear that these are more ambitious; and are attempting to somehow rehabilitate a mute typology that might otherwise be considered post-architectural. The canopies redeem a form for the building, and a scale as well—their massiveness underscores the gigantism of the building more generally. A similar critical optic is anticipated in Jorge Silvetti and Rodofo Machado's proposed Steps of Providence (1978), in which the disarticulated topography and building levels of the Rhode Island School of Design campus are unified, practically and symbolically, by a monumental flight of steps. This element unifies, but also provides an index of the "leftover" character of RISD's urban situation.

Examples of deformation and disproportion expose a counter-intuitive fact: the kinship of distortion and truth. It is often the case that distorted objects—or at least, dysmorphic or disproportionate representations—appear to us as "truer" or more accurate than their respective norms. This is clearly a very ironic outcome: after all, the deformity is understood precisely as the violation of what is either expected or accurate. However, in many contexts (such as caricature, wherein a single feature gains hyperbolic scale or form) the reverse holds. These appear to capture the essence of something precisely by weirding their components and relations. This is because distortion is used as an analytical operation, a way of exposing the importance of less visible qualities.

As mentioned in our introduction, distortion is a powerful de-naturalizing force. It contains within itself a kind of savage Nietzschean laughter, which expels the masks of given-ness from those conventional languages— be they antique or modern—that take certain conventions on faith. It likewise contains the germ of a critical operation, a lens through which the peculiar conditions of architecture might be exaggerated or caricatured. But like many such excoriating forces, the architect must choose a scale of intervention: opting for the general or the specific. VPRO—like OMA's Jussieu Library before it—is ultimately a substitution of saddles for flat slabs, in much the same way that certain "deconstructive" buildings offered an exchange of obliquities for rectitudes. It has an overwhelming aesthetic power, but this force can render subtler formal statements inaudible. Many would find the distortion more threatening when it is more legible. Hence, perhaps, Eisenman's and Cohen's insistence upon the clarity of individual deformative operations. Here, the horror of the dysmorphic becomes an analytical tool, as well as a mode of undermining conventions. It appears, contrary to logic, as both truthful and redemptive.

Postscript

In the previous chapters, we have described a number of specific typologies—we might equally call them "tropes"—that characterize the imaginary of horror: multiplicity and variety, death, misrepresentation, incontinence, disproportion and distortion. These describe points on a spectrum; they hardly exhaust the subject. Earlier drafts of this book also contained chapters on formlessness, dislocation, priapism, simulation, and invasive natures. All of these remain important sub-genres in their own right. Due to constraints, we have selected those which seem most fundamental, or which make for the most compelling introductory survey.

All of these, however, are substantially driven by common economic factors. They also, as we have argued, share an intimate (if occult) relationship to the modern project. We find in them the local effects of a general pressure: a peculiar dynamic that has been called, for lack of a better term, *the geography of unevenness.*

Urban and regional economies give rise to great polarities of wealth, and exercise their own perverse gravity. Discrepancies of value may translate into the radical intensification of some pieces of real estate, and the neglect of others. The maximization of small and expensive sites leads, again, to the creation of new typologies and the necessity of more extreme scales of building—today, again, in much the same manner as the Chicago Loop of the late 19th century. This leads to the problems of hyper-agglomeration on certain sites, and devaluation at others. The city skyline becomes, in effect, a histogram of value.

Polarization unleashes new tendencies and stretches the resources of existing languages. Strange objects appear. We have seen how enlargement and consolidation lead to the horizontal proliferations of the terrace and of Levittown, the gigantism of Solon Beman's grandstand, the Trojan Horse(s) of the opera house and cineplex, or the abysmal interior collage of Mall of America. Such differentials produce other effects in multi-storey commercial structures. As described, hoteliers will tactically render a quantum of floor space un-inhabitable, in order to replace it at a more lucrative position within a finite allocation of square footage. Likewise, landlords in Bonn will abandon second floors in order to realize the price of the stair's footprint at the first level. In the Shanghainese equivalents, invalids are stored in attic gables. Such "decanting" is, in fact, a micro-scale transfer from low- to high-value areas *within* a building, leading to necrotic pockets in its fabric. The resulting ghost-rooms and -floors give rise to their own mythopoetic horrors, to narratives of haunting and strange event. They also birth a horrid object, the vibrant building that is partially ruined.

Certainly, the modern bastard-architectures of cloning, gigantism, and partial death originate here. The market creates such disproportions of value that these become inevitable. And at the same time, such things also become thinkable. Until recently, no resident of Bonn or Shanghai would have tolerated the existence of such unexploited spaces. They are unnerving and wasteful. For the same reasons, no self-respecting Modernist architect or planner would brook dead pockets in the midst of his high street or high rise. Such horrors show the chill penetration of market logic into our lifeworld, and the accommodation of counter intuitive, even unpalatable, consequences.

But equally importantly, the entire spectrum of architectural production adapts to these forces—not merely the crass excrescences of the purely commercial building. Elite design also molts its skin, and becomes something new. Astute observers, such as Rem Koolhaas and Frank Gehry, take the monstrous innovations of business and turn them into high-end polemics and innovative propositions. This is done through practice as well as in essays, such as Koolhaas' "Bigness, or the Problem of Large," which provide a back passage between the theory of the boardroom and that of the atelier.

This is a moment in which another very important relationship becomes visible: how such financial plate-tectonics engage avant-garde practices. If we remove the stylish treatments and the quasi-utopian language of "programming" associated with the Koolhaas's *cadavre exquis*, for example, we are left with something that looks a lot like a mall. The freedoms of the large commercial structure form the deep grammar of an IIT McCormick Tribune Campus Center: its fragmentation, its permissive fabric, its localized environments, and its meandering circulation. This resemblance can be made turbid with appeals to urbanism, Situationism, and the like. In much the same way that OMA's approach emerges from this matrix, Frank Gehry's redeems the calculatedly rumpled picturesque of the pedestrianized mall. Koolhaas may be correct in his claim that Gehry is Jon Jerde's less "evil twin"—just as, by odd reciprocity, Koolhaas may be Victor Gruen's. In the formal mirroring of high and low horror, we are left to wonder if such genius is purely inventive, or whether it performs a sinister ventriloquism. Are these wonderful anomalies the creation of design insight, or the practicum of rentier development? How much of our vanguard re-presents givens as choice?

The study of horror is interesting, perhaps, because it unearths a very precise moment of articulation between economic and artistic practices. The passage from urban geography to *unheimlich* building is one that can be mapped, and it shows how rich a vein of anomaly can emerge from two conjoined processes: polarization among places, and the corollary drift toward monopolization and consolidation.

But here, again, we encounter the ambiguity of horror. It would appear to be a puppet-practice, a superstructural layer built over the grinding plates of typological evolution. But the reality is, luckily, somewhat less simple. Not all of these bastards can be laid full-born at the doorstep of commerce. Again, horror is *in* the moment, but not *of* it. The works of architects are mediated by design intelligence, which contributes its own instabilities and ambivalences.

This can be detected in those projects of Johnston Marklee, Alejandro Aravena and Atelier Bow Wow (above), which incorporate elements that, themselves, resist incorporation into an easy totality. These seem to insist on their slippery conceptual character, in particular their subversive relationship to typological conventions. We would locate a similar deviance in the geometries of a Scott Cohen or a Peter Eisenman, which appear to express a desire to remain unstable and unresolved, open to various interpretations against the specter of a norm. Gehry and OMA express a similar distaste for the utopian whole-ness of an International Style architecture, albeit via very different methods and emphases.

We can locate horror in precisely this tendency, which declines the anodyne. It stubbornly opts to articulate the conditions of its making, to stew in its awkwardness. It does not choose the apparent resolution of the Miesian building—which, it should be noted, leads to its own tensions and ambiguities. The horror is not "good" at abstraction, because its logic pulls in the opposite direction: toward over-articulation and unrestraint. Its materiality, and its formal problematics, seem ever to be pushed back into our line of sight, to be aired in public. This is the effect of the incontinent building, that failed Modernist object that exposes its pipes and wires alongside the trappings of embarrassing interiority. This is likewise true of its "refined" analogue: the Pompidou, Joe Colombo's restaurant at the 14th Milan Triennale, or M. Rokkaku's IS House in Japan. All of these retain, despite their intentionality, the ludic exhibitionism of waggling their tubes *en plein air*. Such vulgar materialism can not be easily domesticated.

Why is this approach useful, or desirable? It is so because it refuses to smooth over the problematic character of contemporary types, those which define the envelope of today's architecture. It forgoes making a virtue of necessity, or using sophisticated devices to make this predicament appealing. And in doing so—more simply—it makes for interesting buildings. What results is not simply an expression, a representational object, or (at worst) a bromide or charming diversion.

This might be contrasted with other design methods, which instead place their emphases on less meaningful kinds of variability, or on the sensational and diaphanous potentials of surface. This is true of the slew of "procedural" architectures, which try to dodge the problems of the contemporary building through the expression of system. The parametric or "scripted" building, when not yoked to a larger idea, is precisely this. The architecture of Jean Gang is a fair example, epitomized in the vacuous visual oscillation of the Aqua Building, in Chicago. This is likewise manifested in an obsession with the effects of shape and material, as in certain works by BIG, Thomas Heatherwick, and Kazuyo Sejima.

These objects appeal to the emotions, in order to—in a very Romantic fashion—bypass the intellect and grasp at some interior being. Horror shares a common history, here, of course. But, unlike some strains of the Picturesque tradition, it has tended to unsettle, to return us to a "graphic" reality, rather than encourage suspension in an affective, post-intellectual ether.

This is the ultimate power of horror, despite its elisions and debasements: the strange humanism found in asserting the post-humanism of its own origins, and in making trouble with its circumstances. It reserves this soft power of bending the rules of type in the service of something other than spectacle. This is where the horrid shares a frontier with the messianic. Through such works, it suggests, the architect might yet, still, survive.

Acknowledgements

Horror in Architecture represents a way of looking at buildings and environments that has been shaped by a number of individuals. In particular, by strong influences from Harvard GSD: Scott Cohen, Luis Rojo de Castro, Hashim Sarkis, Luis Carranza, Toshiko Mori, John Beardsley, Michael Van Valkenburgh, Rodolfo Machado and Jorge Silvetti, Jacques Herzog and Pierre de Meuron. And later, by David Adjaye, Wong Mun Summ, and Richard Hassell.

This book has also benefited from many ongoing conversations with academics and theorists—most of whom had no idea what they were contributing to, so cannot be blamed. We would like to thank Denis Cosgrove, John Agnew, J. Nicholas Entrikin, Achille Mbembe, John and Jean Comaroff, Jane Gordon, and Elizabeth Helsinger. In particular, we would like to thank Lewis Gordon for his insightful read of a massive draft at a critical moment, and for comments that shaped the current version.

We would also like to thank Melanie Lee and Gordon Goff from ORO for their advice and support, and Dolly Foo, Shunann Chen, and Eunice Zhuang for their drawings and assistance.

Image Credits

By page:

10   Courtesy of Mrs. Roberta Cerini Baj, with assistance from Fondazione Marconi

17   Image 1, Philadelphia Museum of Art; purchased with funds contributed by the Daniel W. Dietrich Foundation, 1990 ©Estate of George Paul Thek; photograph: D. James Dee; Courtesy Alexander and Bonin, New York. Images 2 & 3, courtesy of Aeroplastics Contemporary

25   Conway Library, Courtauld Gallery

29   Image 2, courtesy Lucy McRae, Bart Hess, Nick Knight

55   Image 3, courtesy Elemental / Alejandro Aravena Architects; Image 4, courtesy Johnston Marklee

64   Courtesy Bauhaus Archiv

66   Copyright: Bauhaus Archiv / SACK 2012

67   Courtesy FAT

70   Photo: Dick Frank, courtesy Eisenman Architects

71   Courtesy Chicago Historical Society

73   Image 1, Copyright: SACK 2012; Image 2, courtesy Brett Murray

74   Copyright: Andreas Gursky/VG Bild-Kunst/ SACK 2012; Courtesy Sprueth Magers, Berlin & London

77   Copyright: SACK 2012

79   Above, photo: Stephen Hill, courtesy Venturi Scott Brown and Associates, Inc. Below, James Stirling / Michael Wilford fonds, Collection Centre Canadien d'Architecture/ Canadian Centre for Architecture, Montréal

82   Both images, courtesy Gehry Partners, LLP

84   Image 2, courtesy MVRDV. Image 3, courtesy Kris Kuksi.

86   Image 4, courtesy Lucy McRae and Bart Hess

87   Courtesy Henrique Oliveira, Galleria Millan

95   Image 2, copyright: SACK Korea; Image 3, courtesy Filip Dujardin, Highlight Gallery

96   Image 2, courtesy Singapore Biennale.
108   Courtesy, Bernd and Hilla Becher, Sonnabend Gallery
111   Above, courtesy Chicago Historical Society
115   Courtesy Gehry Partners, LLP
124   Below, courtesy, Bernd and Hilla Becher, Sonnabend Gallery
125   Below, courtesy of Chris Dorsey
128   Photo: Jochen Jansen, under CC license
134   Copyright: Frank Relle
142, Image 1: Courtesy of the artist; Image 2: Courtesy of the artist, D'Amelio Gallery, Susanne Vielmetter Gallery. Photo: Josh White
164   Image 2, copyright: SACK Korea
172   Copyright: Darren Soh, Fullframephotos
175   Courtesy, Karezoid / Michal Karcz
176   Image 1, copyright: Reuters/ China Daily Information Corp. Image 2, copyright: Juergen Richter/ Getty Images
178   Image 3, copyright: Jochen Tack / Getty Images
179   Image 4, courtesy Filip Dujardin, Highlight Gallery; Image 5, courtesy Ralph Lieberman
181   Images 1, 2: Takeo Kamiya; Image 3: Paul Glazzard
185   Image 3, courtesy Poelzig Archiv, Architekturmuseum TU Berlin
186   Image 1, courtesy Poelzig Archiv, Architekturmuseum TU Berlin
189   Courtesy Poelzig Archiv, Architekturmuseum TU Berlin
191   ©Antonio López Garcia, VEGAP, 2012.
192   Image 1, photo: Robert Hart, courtesy MVRDV; Image 4, courtesy Gehry Partners, LLP
193   Image 6, © The Estate of Francis Bacon. All rights reserved. DACS 2012
195   Photo: Dick Frank, courtesy Eisenman Architects
196   Image 1, courtesy Lucy McRae and Bart Hess

The author and publisher gratefully acknowledge the permission granted to reproduce the copyright material in this book. Every effort has been made to trace copyright holders and to obtain their permission for the use of copyright material. The authors apologize for any errors or omissions in the above list and would be grateful if notified of any corrections that should be incorporated in future reprints or editions of this book.

NOTES

Introduction

1 In the story "Ligeia." See *The Complete Tales and Poems of Edgar Allan Poe* (New York: Vintage Books, 1975), 655.

2 In "The Marriage of Heaven and Hell" (see below), 186.

3 In *On Ugliness* (1635), excerpted in Umberto Eco, *On Ugliness* (London: Harvill Secker, 2007), 149.

4 Longinus (see note 6) marries the concept to "terror" or fear.

5 Immanuel Kant, *Observations on the Feelings of the Sublime and the Beautiful*, (Berkeley: University of California Press, 1960), 44-6.

6 *Longinus on the Sublime* (Oxford: T&G Shrimpton, 1817), 48.

7 Philip Shaw, *The Sublime*, (London: Routledge, 2006),

8 Ibid., 14.

9 Ibid., 21.

10 Immanuel Kant, *Observations on the Feelings of the Sublime and the Beautiful*, (Berkeley: University of California Press, 1960), 24.

11 See http://www.vam.ac.uk/collections/paintings/galleries/further/essay/romance/index.html#footnotes.

12 Ibid.

13 Joseph Addison, *Remarks on Several Parts of Italy etc. in the years 1701, 1702, 1703.* 1773 edition, printed for T. Walker, 261.

14 See Shaw, 30.

15 In Burke, *On the Sublime and the Beautiful*, "Of the Passion Caused by the Sublime," Part II, Chapter 1.

16 And as such finds itself in the company of science fiction, mystery and crime writing and film, and fantasy/erotica.

17 Adorno would likely not have considered such cultural products to be art, only fetishes. Interview with Adorno, http://www.youtube.com/watch?v=Xd7Fhaji8ow

18 3-D Doritos use a pyramidal form in order to magnify sound in the inner ear. He notes that "at 95 decibels...[teenagers] showed significant increased aggression." Stewart Lee Allen, *In The Devils Garden: A Sinful History of Forbidden Food* (Edinburgh: Canongate, 2002), 225.

19 Georg Simmel, in *Georg Simmel on Individuality and Social Forms* (Chicago: University of Chicago Press, 1971), 324.

20 From "Homer vs. The Eighteenth Amendment," the eighteenth episode of the 8th season of The Simpsons.

21 This opinion of Olivier's was apparently closely modeled on Tocqueville, who was horrified by the American invention. Peter Carey,

Parrot and Olivier in America (London, Faber and Faber, 2010), 357.

22   See Gillo Dorfles, *Kitsch: An Anthology of Bad Taste* (New York: Bell Publishing, 1988), passim.

23   *Seedbed*, enacted January 1971, Sonnabend Gallery, New York City.

24   Kipling also wrote tales of horror. These included works such as "The Recrudescence of Imray," in which a corpse is found in the ceiling of an Indian bungalow. See *Rudyard Kipling's Tales of Horror and Fantasy* (New York: Pegasus Books, 2008).

25   There are many phenomena that strike one as horrible but not uncanny, and vice versa. The unheimlich often presents itself as a sort of creep; horror is more commonly associated with shock.

26   Paul Thek, *Meat Piece with Warhol Brillo Box*, 1965, from the series *Technological Reliquaries*.

27   See Greil Marcus, *Lipstick Traces: A Secret History of the Twentieth Century* (Cambridge: Harvard University Press, 2009). Also Dick Hebdige, *Subculture: The Meaning of Style* (London: Routledge, 1979).

28   Hirst repeats this claim in his monograph, *I Want to Spend the Rest of My Life Everywhere, with Everyone, One to One, Always, Forever, Now* (London: Booth-Clibborn, 2006).

29   It is another case of unrequited passion, a non-appearance of the "real." Such non-appearance is theorized by William Mazzarella in *Shoveling Smoke: Advertising and Globalization in Contemporary India* (Durham NC: Duke University Press).

30   However, it is important to note generic overlaps between crime fiction and horror. The "pulp" novel can be distinguished from detective fiction in its focus on sex and violence. The *Fantômas* series, by Pierre Souvestre and Marcel Allain, for example, were famous for gory details.

31   *The Shock Doctrine: The Rise of Disaster Capitalism* (New York: Picador, 2008).

32   This is a very far-reaching cultural phenomenon. The rise in charismatic movements centered upon ecstatic experience—are discussed in detail in Joshua Comaroff, *Vulgarity and Enchantment: Religious Movements and the Space of the State,* PhD dissertation, University of California Los Angeles, Department of Geography (November, 2009). Among academic works, Davidson, Bondi and Smith's *Emotional Geographies* (2005) is quite typical; a more sophisticated example is Brian Massumi's *Parables for the Virtual* (2002).

33   Throughout *Gargantua and Pantagruel* (London: Penguin Classics, 2006).

34   See John Carpenter's *The Thing*.

35   Hillel Schwartz, *The Culture of the Copy* (New York: Zone Books, 1998), 50.

36   *Ibid.*, 50. The italics are Schwartz's.

37   Kant's statement modifies the lingering classical notion of "unity in multiplicity," which dominated theorization of beauty in his moment. See his *Observations* (cited above, note 10).

38   Robert Mills, "Jesus as Monster," in Bettina Bildhauer and Robert Mills, *The Monstrous Middle Ages* (Toronto: University of Toronto Press, 2003), 39.

39   Barbara Bender, "Stonehenge - Contested Landscapes (Medieval to Present Day), in Bender (ed.), *Landscape: Politics and Perspectives* (Providence, RI: Berg, 1993), 253-4.

40   See Alfred, Lord Tennyson's "The Passing of Arthur," which links the King to Christ. Similar stories originate around the eighth century. In many, Christ himself is crucified on an apple tree, and a "wild apple" representing the Celtic faiths, is nailed to the same tree. See Stewart Lee Allen's *In the Devil's Garden: A Sinful History of Forbidden Food* (Edinburgh: Canongate, 2002); Barbara Catherine Raw, *Anglo-Saxon Crucifixion Iconography and the Art of the Monastic Revival* (Cambridge, Cambridge University Press, 2009).

41   Franco Moretti, *Signs Taken for Wonders* (London: Verso, 2005), 83.

42   Ibid., 84.

43   Schwartz, 56.

44   Moretti, 84.

45   Gang Yue, *The Mouth That Begs: Hunger, Cannibalism, and the Politics of Eating in Modern China* (Durham, NC, Duke University Press, 1999). Also, Mo Yan, *The Republic of Wine* (New York, Arcade Publishing, 2001).

46   Achille Mbembe, *On The Postcolony* (Berkeley, CA, University of California Pres, 2001), 3-8.

47   To use Lovecraft's language. From *The Dunwich Horror*, (London, Penguin, 2008), 175.

48   Julio Cortázar, *Hopscotch* (New York, Pantheon, 1987), 4.

49   See Denis Cosgrove, *Social Formation and Symbolic Landscape* (Madison, WI: University of Wisconsin Press, 1984).

50   Edmund Burke agreed, lamenting Montaigne's need to discuss his masturbation habit. *The New Yorker*, Sept 7, 2009, p.41, "Me, Myself, and I" by Jane Kramer.

52   http://www.kent.ac.uk/secl/journals/skepsi/issues/issue%201/V1%20%281%29,%20Claire%20Lozier.pdf.

53   See Mona Domosh, *Invented Cities: The Creation of Landscape in Nineteenth Century New York and Boston* (New Haven, CT, Yale University Press, 1998).

54   John W. Stamper, *Chicago's North Michigan Avenue: Planning and Development, 1900-1930* (Chicago, University of Chicago Press, 1991), 71.

55   Cf. the Evanston Country Club and the Glen View Club, both by Holabird and Roche, or the Shinnecock Hills Golf Clubhouse, in Long

Island, by McKim, Mead and White Architects.

56   At the very least, the assimilation of the constituent figures is a bit rough around the edges: while the mass conforms roughly to the outline of a (super)human figure, many limbs appear to dangle off the sides.

57   Mies' was not alone in convincingly addressing the problem of the tall building. Hood had realized the power of the neo-Gothic, and its vertical continuities, in organizing windows. Sullivan and others had success with the expression of the frame.

58   Windows are positioned purely as a result of their conceptual distribution, not the locations required by planning.

59   See Colin Rowe, "Chicago Frame," in *The Mathematics of the Ideal Villa and Other Essays* (Cambridge, MA: MIT Press, 1976).

60   See *The City in History* (San Diego: Harvest, 1989), 430.

61   See K. Michael Hayes, *Modernism and the Posthumanist Subject: The Architecture of Hannes Meyer and Ludwig Hilberseimer* (Cambridge, MA: MIT Press, 1992).

62   We are following Anthony Vidler's *The Architectural Uncanny: Essays in the Architectural Unhomely* (Cambridge, MA: MIT Press, 1994).

63   *The Station Hill Blanchot Reader: Fiction and Literary Essays* (Barrytown, NY: Station Hill Press, 1995).

Doubles

1   In "The Marriage of Heaven and Hell," 192.

2   Ibid., 142.

3   See Robert Mills, "Jesus as Monster," in Robert Mills and Bettina Bildhauer, eds, *The Monstrous Middle Ages* (Toronto: University of Toronto Press, 2004).

4   As in, for example, *Cousin Bette* (London: Penguin Classics, 2004).

5   This is perhaps why the semi has been employed less in the U.S., where other forms of mass housing have been more popular.

6   Melville, *Billy Budd, Sailor*, (London: Penguin Classics, 1986), 327.

Clones

1   Freud, *The Uncanny*, 144.

2   Ibid., 158.

3   This concept was introduced in *Thus Spake Zarathustra*.

4   The Georgian rowhouse met with a range of opinions. In his *Georgian Architecture* (London: David & Charles, 1993), James Stevens Curl notes that they were considered "dark and gloomy," as well as typologically indistinct: they might "easily be mistaken for hospitals, arsenals, or public granaries" (186).

5   This might be contrasted with a town, for example, where other civic

structures—town hall, post office, main street—are "public."

6 These can be seen along the streets bounding North Avenue, between Clark Street and the Cybourne Corridor.

7 This term refers to the ornamented style of a community that united migrant Chinese and Malays in urban Singapore and Malaysia.

8 This is less commonly the problem with the wider London Georgian, which can incorporate several bays of windows at its façade.

9 We are aware that this phrase as connoting a romantic notion of "organic community," a kind of *gemeinschaft* that may not actually exist.

10 Schwartz, 51.

11 We refer to Margaret Thatcher's comment that "there is no such thing as society."

12 Bruno Schulz, *The Street of Crocodiles* (London, Penguin, 1992), 32.

13 *Editorial El Croquis* (Madrid), Peter Eisenman, p.51.

14 Ibid., P.60.

Exquisite Corpse

1 Thomas Fuller, *The Holy and Profane States: With Some Account of the Author and His Writings*, (Ann Arbor, MI: University of Michigan Library, Scholarly Publishing Office, 2006), 201.

2 Bruno Schulz, *The Street of Crocodiles* (New York: Penguin Classics, 1992), 69.

3 See Alison Winter, *Mesmerized: Powers of Mind in Victorian Britain* (Chicago: University of Chicago Press, 1998).

4 This is discussed in Gaby Wood's *Living Dolls: A Magical History of the Quest for Mechanical Life* (London: Faber and Faber, 2002), 4-5.

5 http://www.bbc.co.uk/news/entertainment-arts-12429353

6 See Rafael Moneo, *Theoretical Anxiety and Design Strategies in the Work of Eight Contemporary Architects* (Cambridge: MIT Press, 2004); see chapter on OMA / Koolhaas for this discussion, 307ff.

7 Mies' early perspectives used montage to place abstract and "primitive" art. See Terrence Riley and Barry Bergdoll's *Mies in Berlin* (New York: MoMA, 2001), 362.

8 While highly manipulable, the Kunsthal's grid provides an overarching compositional system that ties its various volumes together.

Ungrammatical Body

1 Gogol, "A Terrible Vengeance," in *The Collected Tales of Nikolai Gogol* (London: Granta, 2003), 64ff.

2 This might be contrasted with other approaches, such as that of Luigi Moretti, whose "fast" façades are organized into horizontal stripes to create an impression of speed.

3 That is, a single body containing mis-matched elements. However, the doubling of the conjoined twin has very much to do with two bonded individuals, not so much a "common" body

Partially and Mostly Dead

1 Where man drinks of Christ's blood to gain life eternal, the vampire gains immortality by feeding on humans in an inverted communion.

2 BBC article: http://news.bbc.co.uk/2/hi/americas/3816171.stm

3 For an growing catalogue, consult www.deadmalls.com.

4 Quoted in "The Still Mysterious Enchanter," John Banville, *The New York Review of Books*, July 15-August 18, 2010 (Vol LVII, No.12), 46.

5 The narrator of Poe's "MS. Found in a Bottle" writes that he has "imbibed of the shadow of fallen columns…until my very soul has become a ruin," see *Tales of Mystery and Imagination* (London: Bloomsbury, 2009), 56.

6 The sealing of haunted hotel rooms is discussed in detail (with accounts of managers) in Comaroff, *Vulgarity and Enchantment* (above).

7 This is a sort of perversion of the womb, and fruits appear post-human, like miscarried persons.

8 That organization is New Creation Church, also known as "The Rock," a charismatic megachurch led by Pastor Joseph Prince.

Reiteration and Reflexivity

1 This *mise-en-a-bouche* is particularly brilliant, as "Tonguey" is an articulate entity, in contrast to the mumblemouth who is his host.

2 Predication refers to the naming or classification of an object according to a "typical representative of its attributes," as well as the grouping of objects with similar attributes. See *The Rule of Metaphor: The Creation of Meaning in Language* (London, Routledge, 2006), 155.

3 As it happens, this building appears merely playful; it does not seem pretentious, or to aspire to "high" architecture.

4 See Manuel Gausa et al, *The Metapolis Dictionary of Advanced Architecture* (Barcelona: Actar, 2003), 118.

5 Ibid., 226.

Incontinent Object

1 See also Roy Porter's *London* (cited above), and Robin Evans' classic *Translations from Drawing to Building* (Cambridge, MA: MIT Press, 1997).

2 Herman Melville, *Moby-Dick* (London: Penguin Classics Deluxe Edition, 2010), 409.

3 See Alison Winter, *Mesmerized* (cited above).

4 Ibid., p.120.

5 See Foucault's *Birth of the Clinic: An Archaeology of Medical Perception* (New York: Vintage, 1994). Also in Roy Porter's *Blood and Guts: A Short History of Medicine* (London: Penguin, 2003).

6 It is interesting that indoor plumbing was rejected by the British public until long after it became available. In a BBC series, Lucy Worsley noted that an Elizabethan flush toilet was built by Sir John Harrington, but the device did not become widespread for over 200 years. See http://www.bbc.co.uk/blogs/tv/2011/04/if-walls-could-talk-the-history-of-the-home.shtml

7 Analogously, in his "Figures, Doors, and Passages" (in *Translations from Drawing to Building*, as above), Evans demonstrated a similar process in the compartmentalization of the architectural object, and the internalization of its components. This consisted, in part, of a movement from physical proximity to a regime of regulated privacy and subdivision.

8 See Rowe and Slutzky, "Transparency: Literal and Phenomenal," in *Perspecta* Vol.8 (1963), 45-54.

9 In fact, between utopia and connective networks of all kinds. See Armand Mattelart, "Mapping Modernity: Utopia and Communications Networks" in Denis Cosgrove (ed), *Mappings* (London: Reaktion Books, 1999). This is a lingering association, and has been quite frankly re-embraced in projects such as Bruno Latour's "actor-network theory."

10 Kenneth Frampton, *Modern Architecture: A Critical History* (New York: Thames and Hudson, 2007), 244.

11 This is suggested explicitly, also, in the design of some architectural avant-gardes. It is present, for example, in works by Lebbeus Woods, Daniel Libeskind and Bernard Tschumi. The effect is more alarming when not ersatz, as in the Chinese buildings that were recently inhabited.

12 But it is different from the appearance of holes, and apertures. In those occasions, there is a perforation of skin, a birthing. Incontinence speaks more directly of a failure of social being, an excessive sharing.

13 Poe, Fall of the House of Usher, in *Tales of Mystery and Imagination* (London: Bloomsbury, 2009), 181.

14 Ibid., 196-7.

15 *Rudyard Kipling's Tales of Horror and Fantasy*, (New York: Pegasus Books, 2008), 476.

16 Ibid., 519.

17 See Beck's *Risk Society: Towards a New Modernity* (Thousand Oaks, CA: Sage, 1992), 21.

18 Alan Weisman, *The World Without Us* (New York: Picador, 2008), 215.

19 *Moby-Dick*, 409.

20 Modern witch hunts often equate enchantment with a new global order. See James Siegel, *Naming the Witch* (Stanford: Stanford University Press, 2006); Comaroff, Jean and John L. Comaroff. "Occult Economies and the Violence of Abstraction: Notes from the South African Postcolony." *American Ethnologist* 26, no. 3(1999): 279-301; Geschiere, *The Modernity of Witchcraft: Politics and the Occult in Postcolonial Africa* (Charlottesville: University of Virginia Press, 1997); Mbembe, (cited above).

21 Tower, "The Landlord," *The New Yorker*, September 13, 2010, 67.

22 Rand herself, however, has a strange relationship to continence. While Objectivism held the ideal of monads, her characters never stop talking.

Trojan Horse

1 Anselm Gerhard, *The Urbanization of Opera: Music Theatre in Paris in the Nineteenth Century* (Chicago: University of Chicago Press, 2000).

2 See Gérard Fontaine's monograph, *Charles Garnier's Opéra: Architecture and Exterior Decor* (Paris: Patrimoine, 2000).

3 Preston Scott Cohen, *Contested Symmetries and Other Predicaments in Architecture* (New York: Princeton Architectural Press, 2001).

4 It is an interesting fact that the psychotic commonly appears as unremarkable, as having no qualities and as making no real impression.

5 See Evans, *Translations from Drawing to Building* (London: AA Publications, 2005).

6 *The Human Condition* (Chicago: University of Chicago Press, 1998).

7 An informational sign at the entrance to the hotel makes the claim: "'92% of all hotel guests expect no surprises when entering their rooms.'"

8 Paul Virilio, *Bunker Archaeology* (New York: Princeton Architectural Press, 1994), 168.

9 http://www.divaasia.com/article/2554

10 The scenography of commercial buildings is an obvious example, but there are more peculiar ones—such as mosques in Malaysia that are dressed as Chinese temples to encourage conversion to Islam.

Homunculism & Gigantism

1 Male sperm was long thought to contain tiny pre-humanoids that would grow into the fetus when implanted in the womb. This was typical of analogical theories of conception. Mandrake was known to be poisonous and hallucinogenic, and homunculi assumed to be evil.

2 Marcel Mauss, *A General Theory of Magic* (London: Routledge Classics, 2001).

3 For example, in Let the Right One In (2008), and in Anne Rice.

4 The gate is part of the Shanghai *nongtang* (lane house). See Hanchao

Lu's *Beyond the Neon Lights: Everyday Shanghai in the Early Twentieth Century* (Berkeley: University of California Press, 1999), Chapter 4.

5 This is a common effect of the priapic, also.

6 *Moby-Dick*, in Ishmael's excursis on The Tail, 411.

7 Frampton, *Modern Architecture*, 218.

8 http://muar.ru/eng/exhibitions/2006/exibit_15_12_2006_brazini_en.htm

Solidity & Stereotomy

1 See Klein, 353.

2 Richard E. Etlin, *Symbolic Space: French Enlightenment Architecture and its Legacy* (Chicago: University of Chicago Press, 1996), 42.

3 For example, Sacro Monte di Ghiffa, or Mount Athos.

4 http://www.kamit.jp/07_lycia/liki_eng.htm

5 See Julius Posener, *Hans Poelzig: Reflections on His Life and Work* (Cambridge, MA: MIT Press, 1992).

6 It might be shocking that the desire for substance by some Jewish architects resembled that fueling Hitler's ideology. We would clarify that the work of architectural avant-gardes differed from Nazi neoclassicism.

Distortion & Disproportion

1 Margaret Thatcher described Francis Bacon's work in this way.

2 The special corner of perimeter blocks is common throughout Europe. These may be treated with ornament, curvilinear geometries, etc.

3 This could be compared to OMA's Kunsthal, for example, which is planned with a certain conceptual economy. VPRO feels more like a parking garage with "quirk" elements (Persian carpets and chandeliers) placed scenographically.

Published by ORO editions
Publishers of Architecture, Art, and Design
Gordon Goff: Publisher
www.oroeditions.com
info@oroeditions.com

Copyright © 2013 by ORO editions
ISBN: 978-1-935935-90-2
10 09 08 07 06 5 4 3 2 1 First edition

Graphic Design: Lekker Design
Color Separations and Printing: ORO Group Ltd.
Printed in China.

This book was printed and bound using a variety of sustainable
manufacturing processes and materials including soy-based
inks, acqueous-based varnish, VOC- and formaldehyde-free
glues, and phthalate-free laminations. The text is printed using
offset sheetfed lithographic printing process in (book specific)
color on 157gsm premium matte art paper with an off-line gloss
acqueous spot varnish applied to all photographs.

Library of Congress data: Available upon request

For information on our distribution, please visit our website
www.oroeditions.com